Orchestration

Orchestration
Scores & Scoring

DONALD J. RAUSCHER

MANHATTAN SCHOOL OF MUSIC

THE FREE PRESS OF GLENCOE

COLLIER-MACMILLAN LTD., LONDON

For information, address:

The Free Press of Glencoe
A Division of The Macmillan Company,
The Crowell-Collier Publishing Company
60 Fifth Avenue, New York 11

Collier-Macmillan Canada, Ltd., Toronto, Ontario

Library of Congress Catalog Card Number: 63-8421

Stravinsky: *Firebird Suite* (1919 version), by permission of the copyright owners, J. & W.
Chester, Ltd., London. Hindemith: *Mathis der Maler*, copyright 1934 by B. Schott's Soehne,
Mainz; renewed 1961 by Paul Hindemith; all rights reserved; reprinted by permission of B.
Schott's Soehne, Mainz, the original copyright owner and its U. S. representative, Associated Music
Publishers, Inc., New York. Ravel, *Daphnis and Chloe*, Suite No. 2, permission for reprint granted
by Durand et Cie, Paris; copyright owners: Elkan-Vogel Co., Inc., Philadelphia, agents. Bartok:
Concerto for Orchestra, copyright 1946 by Hawkes & Son (London) Ltd.; reprinted by permission
of Boosey & Hawkes Inc.

Preface

Misconceptions of orchestral organization and procedure are matters of innocent faith with the general public. Too many students of music are led to believe that orchestration, after instrumental ranges and relative dexterities have been thoroughly assimilated, is largely a matter of writing felicitous solo passages. The sanctity afforded the production of the masters has led even some professional musicians to consider their orchestral garb as beyond criticism.

Each of these is a barrier to a true understanding of orchestral music. Ignorant confidence in superficial impressions, dry and mechanical memorization, and the misguided approbation of a scoring technic that shows every sign of being a result of compromise with contemporary instrumental shortcomings are hardly fruitful bases for the acquisition of practical skills.

It is chiefly the distressing awareness of these three conditions that has prompted the writing of this book. The author's views on the subject are as follows:

1. Music, in its truest voice, is a natural means of exclusively human communication.

2. The forms that this natural impulse must take in order to be understood are technical, and the disciplines of music are more numerous and more definable than those of any other art.

3. Orchestration is but one of these disciplines, and its study must be undertaken with a full awareness of the fact that it is not an end or an art in itself.

4. Music is sound, not merely notation and analysis. The study of instruments and their uses is fascinating, but it is sterile unless the vital presence of sounding music constantly governs the process of learning.

An understanding of orchestral vocabulary and the technic of orchestration must be acquired before a score can be simultaneously heard and read. Therefore, Part One of this book attempts to deal with the practical aspects of instrumental usage. Part Two consists of well-known scores, each of which deserves serious study; these scores must be heard, and the discourses that accompany them must be considered only in the light of their sound. The final section offers a variety of clearly defined styles of music to be translated into orchestral sound.

Tradition now requires that the author's debt to others be acknowledged, but if all who aided, directly or indirectly, in the making of this book were to be named it would double in size. My friends and colleagues at Manhattan School of Music, less professional but equally helpful advocates in New Hampshire and New York, and, above all, my wife, Justine, are recipients of my most fervent gratitude.

D. J. R.

New York, December, 1962

To the Teacher

This text is planned to instruct in the three essential areas of orchestral technic: the knowledge of instruments and orchestral organization, the evaluation of extant orchestral literature, and the development of individual scoring skill. Sufficient material for analysis and transcription has been included to make it possible for teachers and students of orchestration to pursue the subject without the constant need to obtain multiple copies of scores and nonorchestral compositions for transcription.

The book is divided into three parts to correspond with these areas of instruction, but they are not intended to be dealt with singly. The studies of Part One and the scoring projects of Part Three may easily be spaced to provide class assignments for two fifteen- or sixteen-week semesters. It will be found that an assignment requiring two or three weeks for completion can be explained in one session. The scores discussed in Part Two should be introduced during the meetings in which no new assignment need be presented and whenever the lesson can be disposed of in less than the alloted class time. Study 12(a), Chapter 7, for example, should not be assigned before Grieg's "Ase's Death," p. 97 (or another clear illustration of bowing technic), has been heard and studied. Similarly, coordination of Parts One and Two are essential.

Supplementary and equally valuable assignments may be made. A report on two or more recorded or actual performances of a work included in Part Two, comparing them with the analysis given, may be required. Term projects, such as a detailed survey of an instrument or instrumental family, a large-scale scoring project of the students' selection, or a critical examination of this and other orchestration texts may be assigned. It is possible to amplify, elaborate, or revise the studies of Part One and to substitute or add works in Parts Two and Three. Each teacher will have personal preferences and inclinations; and these are most certainly to be given full play, for effective teaching is as much a result of teacher enthusiasm as of any other single factor. It is a prime objective of this text to prompt students and teachers to listen to music, to study scores, to delve into original sources of musicological information, and to tap the innermost resources of individual musical conscience. If in the author's analyses of orchestral scores and of piano pieces or in his appraisals of instrumental usage, there should be detected by some a trace of arbitrary opinion, dissent is welcomed. No more profitable educational device exists, and it should not be forgotten that the greatest contributions to musical art were made by individualists.

Competent instrumentalists should be employed to aid in the presentation of the appropriate sections of Part One whenever possible. Excellent recorded demonstrations of individual orchestral instruments are available and should be used when the services of a contra bassoonist, celesta player, or other instrumentalist cannot be had during the class period.

Recorded performances of the scores of Part Two are absolutely indispensable; and if two or more recorded versions of each work can be heard, the value of this aspect of study will be intensified. The works discussed must be heard in actual performance or as recorded, for all verdicts and questions concerning them can be based only upon their sound.

Well-played performances of student scores are valuable, but they are usually impractical because of the large numbers of student orchestrators. Where possible, an arrangement may be made that only the best or most representative work of a given class is prepared for performance.

If no performance is possible, the students should be made aware of the many factors that militate against it even in the best of circumstances. The drudgery of copying parts and the preparation of an accurate and readable conductor's score is frequently enough to discourage students, but there are other deterrents. Student performers are seldom eager to use time that could be devoted to the study of established literature for the convenience of unfinished orchestrators. Even given the most willing orchestra, the best that can usually be had is an unrehearsed reading, which is likely to distort even the most masterful of orchestral works. And finally and inevitably, there is the melancholy fact that, willing or unwilling, a fully manned and competent orchestra is rarely on hand. Performances or not, the teacher must convince the students that only the assiduous study of scores, seen and heard, and the transmutation of the concepts thus absorbed into his own work will result in scoring skill.

A diligent student with only a minimal training in harmony, counterpoint, form, and literature should be able to cope with the requirements of the text; but a strong background in these subjects will aid in this as in all other musical study. The terminology used is common, and students should be required to make use of reference books when amplification is needed.

The study of orchestration cannot be separated from the study of musical style and structure, and the examples included are illustrations of more than scoring technic. Each teacher will determine the extent to which nonorchestral aspects will be stressed, the frequency and content of assignments, the degree to which the sound of music will dominate, and the measure to which the author's intent will be realized—the teaching of music through orchestration, rather than orchestration as an isolated craft.

Contents

Part Two SCORE ANALYSIS

Part Three APPLIED TECHNIC

xii

PART ONE

Preliminaries

1

The Orchestra

*T*HE MODERN SYMPHONIC ORCHESTRA may best be compared to a repertory theater. It must be prepared to present authentic performances of many hundreds of works, written over a period of more than two centuries by representatives of many nations and national and personal concepts. It must adapt itself to wide differences in style and technics of performance: for a single evening's performance may include works of Bach, Berlioz, Borodin, and Britten—products of three centuries and four nations. Such varied programs are in no way unusual.

The orchestral "company" which copes with these demands as a matter of course is a highly trained, highly gifted, and rigidly disciplined corps of performers. To the public, a successful musician is an enigma, whose ability is regarded as a gift of divine beneficence beyond the pale of understanding. It well may be, for even Sigmund Freud was unable to reconcile music with his concept of human psychology. Nevertheless, a musician's skill is the result of many years of laborious and continuous effort, and his discipline is the result of a consciously acquired under-

3

standing of the requirements for the realization of the attainments of the highest form of art. Each member of a professional orchestra is an expert, and the orchestral ensemble is an assembly of expert artists. It is the responsibility of the orchestrator to remember that orchestration is not an art in itself, but a translation of unvoiced music into the most expressive of all mediums of musical utterance.

The instruments that have won a permanent place in the orchestra are those that have proved their ability to meet two criteria. They must contribute an individual and consistently attractive tone color, and they must be capable of taking alternately dominant and accompanying roles in the ensemble without lessening the effect of any other instrument. Those which meet these requirements are violins, violas, violoncellos, double basses, flutes, oboes, clarinets, bassoons, horns, trumpets, trombones, tubas, various percussion instruments, and harps. Some of these instruments bring with them under or oversized replicas of themselves: piccolo, alto flute, English horn, E♭ clarinet, bass clarinet, and contra-bassoon are the companions of the flute, oboe, clarinet, and bassoon.

The piano, most popular of all instruments, is not admitted to the orchestra except as a percussion instrument, for a direct juxtaposition with the versatility of the other instruments makes its lack of a true legato embarrassingly evident. Saxophones, guitars, accordions, and other more limited instruments are admitted only when one or the other of their special qualities is used—usually in solo and very rarely—for they do not meet the. two basic conditions of membership.

The pipe organ is a borderline case. It is certainly capable of every gradation of nuance and has a large variety of tone colors at its disposal. It is the most nearly orchestral instrument controlled by a single performer. There are two decisive reasons for its absence in the normal symphonic group. First, it is not always available in the auditoriums in which orchestras perform. Its untransportable bulk means its presence cannot be taken for granted. Secondly, its massive character tends to overawe the orchestra as well as the audience. No other sound can more effectively conjure up a liturgical atmosphere, but a liturgical atmosphere in a nonliturgical situation (as in the majority of musical situations) is distracting. The few instances of its use are a result of the orchestrator's desire either to utilize its ecclesiastical affiliation, overwhelm the listeners with sheer sound, or, as an organist, show his knowledge of and affection for the instrument.

A third condition for orchestral employment now suggests itself. All orchestral instruments (with the possible exception of some members of the percussion family) are dependent for their tone quality upon the physical and mental efforts of a human being. The organ, all electronic devices, the vibraphone, and all electrically amplified sounds rely on an extrahuman apparatus for their tone quality; and it is perhaps this fact which renders them generally unacceptable to the symphonic ensemble. Although many fascinating experiments in sound are presently under way, it remains to be seen whether purely mechanically produced sounds can win a place in the orchestra. At the present time the orchestral literature, the fruit of the inspiration of the established masters of our profession, has been and remains almost unanimously limited to the instruments indicated as members.

Orchestras vary in size according to budgetary considerations and the inclination of their managements. Most include usually more and rarely less than twenty violins, divided into roughly equivalent sections of firsts and seconds. Eight to twelve each of violas and cellos and six to eight double basses complete the string section.

The woodwinds are represented by three or four members of each family. There may be as many as seven or as few as five horns, three to five trumpets, and three or four trombones, but only one tuba. One harpist is usually on the payroll, but the telephone number of a second harpist is usually in the orchestra manager's pocket. One timpanist and two or three other percussionists complete the roster of regularly employed instrumentalists.

This assemblage is equipped to perform the vast bulk of orchestral literature, but some of the instrumentalists are often idle. Many early orchestral works for instance, include parts for only one flute, and have no clarinet parts at all. Trombones are frequently omitted. The tuba appears only in works of the past hundred years or so, and percussion other than timpani are quite rare in the classical repertoire.

Composers have always had to limit themselves to the available instruments, and at the same time score for those necessary to express their musicality. Their solutions to this dilemma have resulted in the fact that very few present-day concert programs require the complete orchestral personnel.

If a program including Brahms' First Symphony, Grieg's Piano Concerto, and Debussy's *Three Nocturnes* were being prepared, the orchestra manager would arrange a rehearsal schedule and plan for the performers to be present as follows:

All the string players at all rehearsals.
Two flutes for the Brahms and the Grieg, three for the Debussy. In the
    Grieg score the second flute plays piccolo for a few measures; in the
    Debussy, the third flute must double on piccolo. The manager there-
    fore thinks of his available players: A is the principal and will be first

5

flute in all three scores, B is normally second flute but does not play piccolo very often, C plays piccolo more often than flute.
Two oboes and two clarinets in each score, English horn in the Debussy.
Two bassoons in the Symphony and the Concerto, three in the *Nocturnes*, contra-bassoon only in the Brahms.
Four horns in each.
Two trumpets for the Brahms and Grieg, three for the Debussy.
Three trombones in each, tuba in the Debussy only.
Timpani in all three, one additional percussionist in the Debussy.
Two harps and eight soprano and eight mezzo-soprano voices for the Debussy *Nocturnes*.

The parts for first horn and first trumpet are so demanding that they require the attention of two players each, the principal and an assistant. In wealthy orchestras with heavy schedules of performance the first trombonist and the third horn player are also provided with assistants, and an alternate first player may be employed for each of the woodwinds.

The manager notes that the bass clarinet player will not take part in this concert, nor will the second percussionist. If the bassoon section includes four players, all will be used; but if, as is usual, there are two bassoons and one contra-bassoon available, the last player will double on bassoon and take the third part in the Debussy. A second harpist and sixteen singers must be found, and the rehearsal schedule must be arranged so that these performers, and the soloist in the concerto, are not required to stand idly by while the orchestra rehearses the Brahms symphony.

The assistant and alternate first wind players may play the concerto while the principal players retire to the wings. This is a not uncommon practice in the larger orchestras, for these players are secondary only in terms of orchestral organization; they are performers of the highest standard.

After considering and deciding upon these and more details, the manager notifies all concerned of the schedule. The conductor is, of course, consulted on all musical matters.

The arrangement of the orchestra on the stage has varied over the years. During the seventeenth century the conductor sat at a harpsichord in the center of the group, more or less haphazardly surrounded by the rest of the ensemble. In the eighteenth century, whether for reasons of changing musical style, greater control, or personal safety, the conductor moved from the harpsichord to the first violin, where his ghost remains as the modern concertmaster. The abandoned harpsichord then disappeared from the orchestra.

At the present time there are at least two seating plans in general

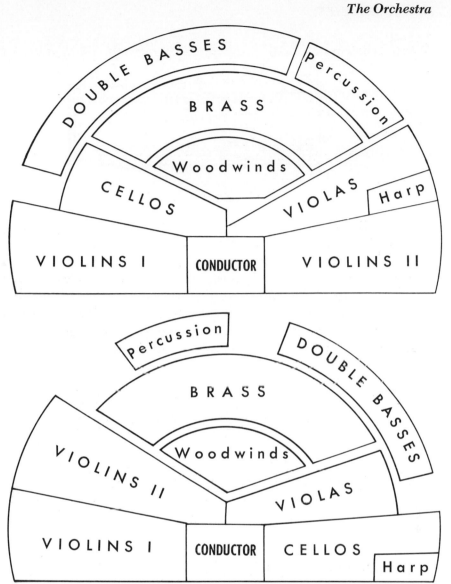

use. The essential difference between the two arrangements is in the location of the second violins, cellos, and double basses. Flutes, oboes, clarinets, and bassoons seem to be universally and permanently assigned to the center of the group directly in front of the conductor, with the horns behind them. Other brass instruments, percussion, and harps are usually placed as shown; but they are subject to many other locations, depending upon the physical properties of the stage, acoustical properties of the hall, and the whim of the conductor. Choosing between these two arrangements is difficult, for in each something is gained and something else is lost.

When Tchaikovsky's Sixth Symphony is played, the passage beginning

EXAMPLE 1

will surely sound better if the first and second violins are on opposite sides of the stage. When the second violins are on the conductor's right, their instruments are tilted away from the audience and the tone is directed toward the back of the stage, while the tone of the first violins, is thrown directly out to the audience. Although the difference is slight, undoubtedly this alternation of full and less full tones on the F♯, E, D, C♯, B, C♯ melody was the composer's intention—no other reason presents itself.

Contrariwise, if the piece at hand is Ravel's Second *Daphnis and Chloe Suite*[1] this passage

EXAMPLE 2

requires a consistent quality of tone and will be more effective if the first two sections of violins are grouped together on the conductor's left.

In general, the first plan is more effectively employed for older scores, in which the first and second violins are roughly equivalent to soprano and alto voices; the second is usually preferable for more modern works, which frequently use the violins as a single mass. It may be mentioned that the added richness of second-violin tone in the second arrangement is by itself enough to convince many of its superiority.

An opera or ballet orchestra must usually be fitted into the pit of the theater. The brass and percussion are usually moved to the far end of the pit at the conductor's right; but perhaps it is safer to say only that under these circumstances the first violins remain at the conductor's left.

---

1. See p. 230 for this passage in context.

2

Orchestral
Instruments

RANGES AND NOTATION

T HE RANGES GIVEN HERE are almost absolutes. Few instruments operate at peak efficiency at the extremities of their ranges, and even though one more higher tone may be squeezed out of many instruments, it is folly to consider the highest or lowest tones given here as equal in tone quality and availability to the ranges used in the scores included in Part Two. Musical notation is used in these definitions with misgivings. Such a portrayal is similar in effect to a map of the United States showing only the east and west coast lines although the subject of study is the terrain between.

1. VIOLIN
Range: From G below middle C to E six leger lines above treble clef.

9

Notation: Treble clef. Nontransposing.

2. VIOLA

Range: From C below alto clef to E three leger lines above treble clef.

Notation: Alto clef. When part lies high, treble clef may be used.

Nontransposing.

3. VIOLONCELLO

Range: From C below bass clef to A one leger line above treble clef.

Notation: Normally bass clef. When part lies on D and A strings, tenor clef may be used. Treble clef for exceptionally high parts.

Nontransposing.

4. DOUBLE BASS

Range: From E four leger lines below bass clef to D one leger line above bass clef.

Notation: The double bass sounds one octave below written pitch; parts are written in the bass clef one octave above actual pitch.

5. FLUTE

Range: From middle C to C three octaves above. C♯ and D above the high C are possible, but rarely used. B below middle C is available on many modern instruments.[1]

Notation: Treble clef. Nontransposing.

6. PICCOLO

Range: From D on the fourth line of the treble clef to the highest C on the piano.

Notation: The piccolo sounds one octave above written pitch; parts are written in the treble clef one octave below actual pitch.

7. ALTO FLUTE (Flute in G)

Range: From G below middle C to G four leger lines above the treble clef.

Notation: The alto flute sounds a perfect fourth below written pitch; parts are written in the treble clef a perfect fourth above actual pitch.

---

1. The low C♯ and C are extensions of the fundamental flute scale. They are obtained by the addition of a foot joint, a short extension of the tube, to the classical length of the instrument. Many modern players use a foot joint long enough to produce B as well, not only because it extends the range downward, but also because it provides another fundamental from which high (third octave) harmonics can be obtained.

8. OBOE

Range: From Bb below middle C to F three leger lines above the treble clef. Chromatics to A above are possible but rarely used.

Notation: Treble clef. Nontransposing.

9. ENGLISH HORN (Cor Anglais)

Range: From E below middle C to Bb one leger line above the treble clef.

Notation: The English horn sounds a perfect fifth below written pitch; parts are written in the treble clef a perfect fifth above actual pitch.

10. CLARINET in Bb

Range: From D below middle C to F three leger lines above the treble clef. Chromatics to Bb above are possible but rarely used.

Notation: The Bb clarinet sounds a major second below written pitch; parts are written in the treble clef a major second above actual pitch.

11. CLARINET in A

> *Range:* From D♭ below middle C to E three leger lines above the treble clef. Chromatics to A above are possible but rarely used.

> *Notation:* The A clarinet sounds a minor third below written pitch; parts are written in the treble clef a minor third above actual pitch.

12. CLARINET in E♭

> *Range:* From G below middle C to B♭ five leger lines above the treble clef.

> *Notation:* The E♭ clarinet sounds a minor third above written pitch; parts are written in the treble clef a minor third below actual pitch.

13. BASS CLARINET in B♭

> *Range:* From D one leger line below the bass clef to F on the top line of the treble clef.

> *Notation, French system:* The bass clarinet sounds a major ninth below written pitch; parts are written in the treble clef a major ninth above actual pitch.

Notation, German system: The bass clarinet sounds a major second below written pitch; parts are written in the bass clef a major second above actual pitch.

The French system of notation is usually preferred by American performers.

14. BASSOON

Range: From B♭ two leger lines below the bass clef to E in the fourth space of the treble clef.

Notation: Nontransposing. Parts are written in the bass clef, or, if chiefly in the upper octave of the range, in the tenor clef.

15. CONTRA-BASSOON

Range: From B♭ six leger lines below the bass clef to F on the fourth line of the bass·clef. Higher tones are possible; but they are ineffective and are rarely used.

Notation: The contra-bassoon sounds one octave below written pitch; parts are written in the bass clef one octave above actual pitch.

16. FRENCH HORN (horn in F)[2]

Range: From B two leger lines below the bass clef to F on the top line of the treble clef. Pedal tones down to G three leger lines below the bass clef are possible, but they are rarely used.

---

2. Horns and trumpets in other keys are common in pre-twentieth-century scores, but all modern instrumental parts are written as given here. (See Chapter 4.)

Notation: The horn in F sounds a perfect fifth below written pitch; parts are written in treble clef a perfect fifth above actual pitch. The bass clef is used when the part lies in the lowest octave. Key signatures are not normally used and all chromatic tones are written as accidentals.

17. TRUMPET in B♭[2]

    Range: From E three leger lines below the treble clef to C two leger lines above the treble clef. Higher tones are possible, but are rarely used.

    Notation: The B♭ trumpet sounds a major second below actual pitch; parts are written in the treble clef a major second above actual pitch.

18. TRUMPET in C[2]

    Range: From F♯ three lines below the treble clef to D two leger lines above the treble clef.

    Notation: Treble clef. Nontransposing.

19. TROMBONE (Tenor Trombone)

    Range: From E one leger line below the bass clef to B♭ on the second leger line above the tenor clef. Higher tones are possible but rarely used.[3]

---

3. The classical trombone section consisted of one alto, one tenor, and one bass trombone. Modern trombonists prefer to use two tenors and a bass because of the richer tone quality. Since the first trombonist is frequently called upon to play alto trombone parts he must extend his range up to E and F above the normal tenor trombone range, but the modern orchestrator gains little more than the contempt of the players if the tenor trombone range is exceeded.

Notation: Nontransposing. Parts are written in the bass clef, or, if chiefly in the upper octave of the range, in the tenor clef.

20. BASS TROMBONE

Range: From C two leger lines below the bass clef to B♭ on the second leger line above the tenor clef. B♮ and B♭ below the low C are possible but rarely used.

Notation: Bass clef. Nontransposing.

21. TUBA

Range: There are various tubas in use. The range most commonly available is from F four leger lines below the bass clef to G three leger lines above the bass clef.

Notation: Bass clef. Nontransposing.

22. HARP

Range: From C♭ five leger lines below the bass clef to G♭ six and one-half octaves above.

Notation: Nontransposing. The great staff is used, as for the piano.

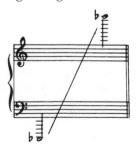

23. TIMPANI (Kettledrums)

Range: It is exceptional when four drums are available. Numbers 2 and 3 are the usual classical complement. Numbers 1, 2, and 3 are common in more recent scores. Number 4 is used only rarely.

1. From D below the bass clef to A a fifth above.
2. From F below the bass clef to C a fifth above.
3. From Bb on the second line of the bass clef to F a fifth above.
4. From D on the third line of the bass clef to A a fifth above.

Notation: Bass clef. Nontransposing.

24. CELESTA

Range: From middle C to the highest C on the piano.

Notation: The celesta sounds one octave above written pitch; parts are written on the great staff one octave below actual pitch.

25. GLOCKENSPIEL

Range: From G above the treble clef to the highest C on the piano.

Notation: The glockenspiel sounds two octaves above written pitch; parts are written in the treble clef two octaves below actual pitch.

17

26. XYLOPHONE

Range: Lowest tone is F in the first space in the treble clef. Highest tone is two and one-half octaves (to C), three octaves, or three and one-half octaves (to C) above, depending on the size of the individual instrument.

Notation: The xylophone sounds one octave above written pitch; parts are written in the treble clef one octave below actual pitch.

27. PERCUSSION INSTRUMENTS OF INDETERMINATE PITCH (snare drum, tenor drum, bass drum, cymbals, wood blocks, tambourine, castanets, triangle, temple blocks, etc.)

Notation: The five line staff is not required and single lines are provided on printed score paper. If a five line staff is used the instrument assigned to each line or space must be clearly and consistently indicated.

The instruments described below are not regular members of the orchestral ensemble, but they are included here for the sake of completeness. Their use in any of the projects in Part Three is not recommended for the reasons given in Chapter I.

28. GUITAR

Range: From E below the bass clef to A above the treble clef. The six strings are tuned, from lowest to highest, to E, A, D, G, B, and E.

Notation: The guitar sounds one octave below the written pitch; parts are written one octave above actual sound.

29. SAXOPHONE

Notation: All saxophones have a written range that extends from
Bb or Bh below the treble clef to E or F three leger lines above
the treble clef. All are transposing instruments.

Range: Soprano in Bb: From Ab two leger lines below the treble
clef to Eb three leger lines above the treble clef. Sounds a
major 2nd below written pitch.

Alto in Eb: From Db on the third line of the bass clef to Ab
above the treble clef. Higher tones are possible but rarely
used. Sounds a major 6th below written pitch.

Tenor in Bb: From Ab in the lowest space in the bass clef to
Eb in the uppermost space in the treble clef. Higher tones are
possible but rarely used. Sounds a major 9th below written
pitch.

Baritone in Eb: From Db below the bass clef to G on the
second line of the treble clef. Many modern instruments extend the range to C two leger lines below the bass clef
(written A two leger lines below the treble clef), and to Ab
in the second space of the treble clef (written F three leger
lines above the treble clef). Sounds an octave and major 6th
below written pitch.

Bass in Bb: From Ab three leger lines below the bass clef to
D one leger line above the bass clef. Sounds two octaves and
a major second below written pitch.

3

Orchestral

Instruments

TECHNICALITIES

*T*HE CASUAL OBSERVER notices that when the percussionist strikes the smaller bars on his xylophone, he produces a high pitch, and when he strikes the larger ones, the tone is pitched lower. Should this listener be so daring as to place a finger on one of the bars as soon as it is struck he would feel the bar shiver. He would then be well on his way to-understanding the principles of tone production in orchestral instruments.

Stringed, woodwind, and brass instruments produce pitch and tone by means of vibrating strings and air columns of controllable length. The instruments that support and enclose these vibrating bodies are so refined and firmly entrenched in our everyday existence that it is easy to overlook their dependence upon basic obvious principles. In the hands of skilled performers they regularly deliver such beautiful sounds that the earth-bound origin of their existence is obscured, but it is the obligation of the orchestrator to know them as thoroughly as the skilled mechanic knows machinery.

20

Much has been written about these instruments; detailed and accurate information on their technical aspects is available to all interested parties, and purple prose describing their tone qualities is everywhere. Only a basic and generalized description of the mechanics of instrumental operation will be given here, for it is impossible to describe adequately their vital presence with words. The technical aspects—problems of fingering, bowing, and blowing—can be really understood only by those who play, therefore, what follows is intended only to impart to those who do not play a proper respect for those who do.

The basic, inescapable factor for all musical sound is the harmonic series. A natural phenomenon of importance to all, is the fact that any sounded tone simultaneously produces other, higher pitched tones. These higher tones are constant and fixed; they are called harmonics, upper partials, or overtones. Tone quality—the difference between the sound of a trumpet and an oboe, for instance—is dependent upon the presence or absence, and the relative strength, of the various harmonics in the fundamental sound. The harmonics are largely responsible for the range and versatility of brass and woodwind instruments, and they are also very important to the technic of stringed instruments.

It must be remembered that the harmonics sound simultaneously with the fundamental. The following example shows the series[1] as it is constituted over the fundamentals C, E, and G.

Play these series of tones on the piano with the sustaining pedal depressed. They sound consonant in spite of the major and minor seconds. Then play any series of random ascending tones in the same way and listen to the harsh dissonances that emerge afterward. This should prove the validity of the harmonic series as a manifestation of physical law in music.

The string or air column vibrates at its full length for the fundamental. Simultaneously it divides in half and these halves themselves vibrate to produce harmonic number 2; in thirds, which vibrate to produce harmonic number three; in fourths, which vibrate to produce harmonic number 4; and so on beyond the sixteenth, which is the highest harmonic used by an orchestral instrument.

The points at which the vibrating segments intersect (the halfway point for harmonic number 2; one-third and two-thirds of the length for harmonic number 3; one-fourth, one-half and three-fourths for number 4 and so on) are called *nodes*.

Brass instruments are the most obvious examples of the harmonic

---

1. Some of these harmonics, particularly numbers 5, 7, and 11, are not in tune according to contemporary standards.

series. The familiar Boy Scout or military bugle demonstrates the principle most clearly. The sound of bugle calls is easily recalled, and the limited number of pitches used is obvious. The bugle is a tube of metal sufficiently long to make available a desired fundamental, and the diameter of the tube is such as to emphasize harmonics number 3, 4, 5, 6 and, less frequently, 2. "Reveille," "Chow," "Taps," and all other bugle calls are composed of these few pitches.

EXAMPLE 3

Horns, trumpets, trombones, and tubas utilize the series in the same way, but are able to produce a greater number of harmonics and can, by the use of valves or slides, change their fundamentals. They are manufactured in various sizes, and the length of the tube is indicated by the key-name of the instrument: for example, B♭ trumpet, C trumpet, F horn, C tuba, F tuba. Each tube is flared at one end to magnify and broadcast the tone, and at the other end is fitted with a cup-shaped mouthpiece against which the player cushions his lips. By tensing and relaxing and by increasing and decreasing the flow of air into the tube the player can evoke harmonics number 1 through 9 and in some instruments even higher ones. These harmonics sound with all the authority and clarity of fundamentals of the same pitch; and in fact, each tone sounded produces

22

its own harmonic series and gives to the instrument its characteristic flavor. It is the player's lips that vibrate to produce tone in brass playing, and the higher the harmonic the greater the demand on the player's physical and musical (primarily intonation) resources.

The valves connect additional tubing to the named length. On all three-valve instruments the middle valve lowers the fundamental by a half step, the first valve lowers it by a whole step, and the third valve lowers the fundamental a step-and-a-half. The combination of the second and third valves lowers the fundamental by two steps, first and third by two-and-a-half steps, and first, second, and third by three steps.

A trumpet in C, for example, when no valve is depressed, is long enough to produce C one octave below middle C, but its diameter is not great enough to accommodate a vibrating air column of such length. The low C is useful only as a fundamental (brass players refer to it as a *pedal tone*) from which, by employing various degrees of lip tension, harmonics numbered 2, 3, 4, 5, 6, 7, 8, and 9 are obtained.

EXAMPLE 4

Since harmonic number 7 is flat in pitch the trumpet player avoids it, and produces B♭ as the eighth harmonic over the pedal B♭, obtained when the first valve is depressed. His complete repertoire of pitches is as follows:

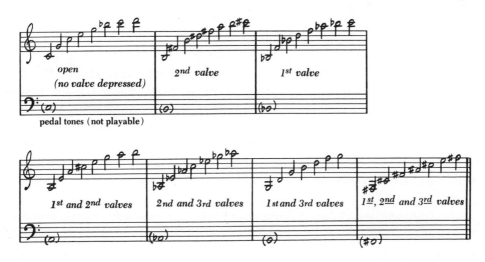

EXAMPLE 5

23

(The harmonic series is infinite and it is possible to force higher tones out of trumpets and other instruments, but the true trumpet tone is lacking and accurate intonation becomes much more difficult when the given range is exceeded.)

All valved brass instruments are equipped this way, although they differ in mouthpiece design, length, diameter, formation of the tube and mouthpiece, and the shape of the bell. Although trombones use a slide instead of valves to change the length of the tube they utilize the harmonic series in the same way.

The tenor trombone has as its first pedal tone the B♭ one octave below the first pedal tone of the B♭ trumpet, and there are seven positions of the slide corresponding to the seven valve combinations.[2] First position on tenor trombone is equal to open position on the valved instruments, second position to second valve position, third position to first valve position, and so on to the seventh position, where the slide is extended to maximum length.

The modern bass trombone is a tenor trombone with larger mouthpiece, bore, and bell, and with additional tubing visible behind the player's left ear when the instrument is in playing position. This additional tubing may be connected to the main tube by means of a valve or switch controlled by the player's left thumb, a switch usually called the "trigger." When so connected, the added tubing lowers the fundamental from B♭ to F. First position then produces F below the lowest line of the bass clef instead of the B♭ above; second position produces E and so on, to the sixth position which produces C. There are only six positions on the longer tube because of the wider spaces between the half-step slide positions.

Most modern horn players use a double horn in F and B♭, actually two instruments in one. The instrument consists of two tubes, one long enough to produce F four leger lines below the bass clef and extendable, with valves, down to the B a diminished fifth lower. The B♭ part of the horn is a tube whose fundamental is B♭ two leger lines below the bass clef; the valves lower it to E. The lowest playable tones are the second harmonics of these fundamentals plus a few not very practical pedal tones on the B♭ horn. A thumb lever effects instantaneous transition from B♭ to F and F to B♭ horns; both divisions use the same three-valve control levers, mouthpiece, and bell. The chief advantage of this instrument lies in the fact that a difficult high harmonic on the F horn can be played on

---

2. Trombones with valves replacing the slide have been constructed but have never been accepted as suitable for orchestral use. The refinements of intonation possible when the length of the tube is directly controlled by the player are not possible with the valved instrument, and the broad purity of tone typical of symphonic trombones is considerably lessened.

the B♭ horn as a lower numbered harmonic. The actual sound of C above middle C for example, is the twelfth harmonic of the F horn, but only a ninth harmonic of the B♭ horn.

Woodwinds use the harmonic series in a slightly different manner. Flutes, oboes, clarinets, and bassoons are also tubes, like the brass; but their tubes are perforated by holes which may be opened or closed by a key mechanism. The flute, for example, is a tube long enough to sound middle C. When the tube is gradually shortened by successively opening the holes beginning at the far end of the instrument, a chromatic scale may be sounded from middle C to C♯ thirteen semitones above, when the tube is at its shortest length. In order to produce higher tones the flutist "over-blows" the lower octave; that is, by slightly altering the embouchure he sounds the second harmonic of each of the tones of the first octave, D to C♯. Thus he has available twenty-six pitches using fourteen basic fingerings.

EXAMPLE 6

Tones above the high C♯ are also obtained by overblowing tones of the fundamental octave, using more or less modified fingerings. Harmonics numbered 3, 4, 5, and 6 are used; high D is the third harmonic of G, E♭ is the fourth harmonic over the fundamental E♭, the high B is a fifth harmonic over G. The choice of fundamental is made according to the availability of those tone holes, essentially located to accommodate the fundamental octave, which are best situated to help in the production of the harmonic.

The oboe and the bassoon function in approximately the same way—each possesses a fundamental scale which is overblown at the second harmonic to sound the second octave; a rather complicated system of fingering to sound a third octave consisting of harmonics higher than the second; and a few extra tone holes and keys to extend the range below the fundamental scale. The oboe's fundamental scale begins on D as does the flute's; the bassoon's begins on G.

The clarinet is the peculiar member of the woodwind family. It is similar to the other woodwinds, with two exceptions. Its first oddity lies in the fact that players of the other woodwinds overblow the fundamental scale to sound the second harmonic; butthe the clarinetist overblows his fundamental scale to sound the *third* harmonic. The second difference is

25

that although the tube of the clarinet is practically the same length as those of the flute and oboe, its lowest tone is almost an octave lower. Both these conditions are primarily due to the clarinet's conical tube, and illustrate an acoustical phenomenon which is too involved to be entered into here.

The woodwinds differ drastically among themselves in the way they set their air columns in motion. The breath of the flutist sets the air in the tube in motion; the clarinetist uses a cane reed to vibrate the air column; and the oboe and bassoon players use double reeds—two strips of cane tied together—for the purpose.

In the stringed instruments, air columns are replaced by strings, and the bow replaces reeds and the flow of breath. Each of these instruments is equipped with four strings tuned as follows:

Double Bass music is written an octave higher than the actual sound for ease of reading and writing.

EXAMPLE 7

With the fingers of the left hand (violinists and violists do not use the thumb) and the bow, held by the right, they produce a fabulous quantity and quality of musical effects. The left hand controls the length of the strings and also supplies a vibrato; the bow arm controls volume, articulation, and nuance. Volume is determined by the speed with which the bow moves on the string and the degree of pressure exerted. Articulation is obtained by stops and starts and changes of direction of the bow. Nuance is a result of the subtle and highly skilled application of these basic technics. Commonly used orchestral bowings are illustrated in Example 8.

EXAMPLE 8

1. Down-bow, up-bow, down-bow, up-bow. When no other indication is given, each tone is given a bow stroke. The term *down beat* is synonymous with *down-bow* in string practice so that it is not necessary to indicate the direction of the bow motion.

2. All four tones are produced on the down-bow. The slurs in string music represent the bowing, not phrasing.

    3. Down-bow on C and D, up-bow on E and F.

(Grieg's *Death of Ase* clearly illustrates these three simple bowing indications.)

    4. All four tones are produced on the down-bow, but the bow is stopped after each tone is sounded, shortening their duration.

    5. Staccato. Alternating bow strokes of short duration.

    6. Tremolo. Very rapid alternation of strokes.

(These three technics can be seen in Schubert's *Unfinished* Symphony. Number 4 is applied in the violas, measure 42; number 5 in measure 77-84; and number 6 in measure 63.)

There are other bowings in the string player's repertoire, but most of them are only exceptionally indicated in an orchestral score.

The strings may be activated by the fingers instead of by the bow. The term used for this is *pizzicato;* the return to the use of the bow is indicated by *arco.* Violas, cellos, and double basses provide a pizzicato bass to the opening of Schubert's *Unfinished* Symphony, and all the strings are pizzicato in the passage beginning in measure 106.

Two, three, or four tones may be sounded more or less simultaneously by string players; but in orchestral playing double, triple, or quadruple stopping, as it is called, it used for chiefly percussive effect. In solo and chamber works it is not unusual, but in the orchestra, where there are many instrumentalists to each part, there is rarely a need for each to produce two or more tones for harmonic reasons.

By reducing the left hand technic to its barest essentials, this phase of string playing may be made clear. Consider a taut string—let us assume it is a violin D string. In order to sound pitches other than D the player must shorten its length by stopping the string between the nut and the bridge. The points at which the finger stops the string for the tones of the scale are shown by the intersecting dotted lines:

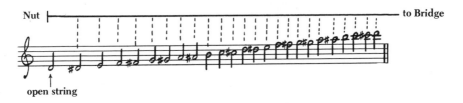

EXAMPLE 9

Notice that the distance between tones becomes smaller as the pitch ascends. Transposition of this illustration down a fifth to G, up a fifth to

A and up a ninth to E will show the complete violin repertoire of pitches.[3]

All the pitches thus shown must be controlled by four fingers of the player's left hand. When string players say "first position," or "third position," they are referring to their method of dealing with this wide range. When the hand is at the nut, the ridge at the upper end of the neck, the fingers can reach, on the D string, E, F, G, and A. This is the first position. In the second position the hand is shifted closer to the bridge and the fingers can reach F, G, A, and B. Higher positions—meaning when the hand is closer to the bridge—render higher pitches available because the fingers can stop the string at increasingly shorter lengths. Accidentals are played by the finger which would normally play the natural of the same letter.

Needless to say, violas, cellos, and double basses use essentially the same method of fingering.

Cellists are fortunate in being able to use the thumb in addition to the other fingers. This is possible because of the relatively easy position in which the instrument is held while playing. Double bass players can employ the thumb position only in the highest register.

There is nothing similar to the woodwind fingering charts available to string players, for most pitches can be obtained from more than one string. The simple figure

EXAMPLE 10

presents three alternatives. All three tones may be played on the G string; only the C may be played on the G string and the A and G on the D string; or three strings may be used: the G string for C, the open A string, and the D string for G. The following diagrams of the violin fingerboard show the positions of the fingers in each arrangement:

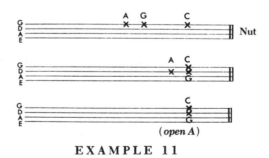

EXAMPLE 11

---

3. Harmonics can be sounded at higher pitches but are not to be considered as readily available and wholly satisfactory range-extenders.

The first example, in which the three tones are played on the G string, requires a shift of position, for the interval of the sixth (C up to A) exceeds the extent to which the fingers can comfortably reach in this register. The shift may be noticeable to the listener as a slight *glissando,* and would be used only if its idiomatic execution or the tone color of the low string were particularly desired. The second example, requiring the smooth transition of the bow from the G to the D string, would normally be the first choice of the player. The third example includes the open A string and would probably not be used except in highly exceptional circumstances. If, however, these three tones are to be played simultaneously the three-string version is the only one possible.

Similar and more complicated situations are the string player's daily fare.

Double, triple, and quadruple stops occur frequently in orchestral music, but, as previously mentioned, usually for percussive effect rather than for harmonic reasons. This effect is obtained by the force with which the bow must move on the strings.

Beethoven's Third Symphony begins with this string effect, and the following examples are taken from the first movement of that work.

EXAMPLE 12

Diagramming the fingerboard as in Example 11 will show the reason for spacing the chords in open position. It should also be noted that such chords are usually surrounded by rests. Consecutive chords are infrequent, but if used, should require a minimum of finger movement. Chords for orchestral cello do not occur nearly as frequently as for violin and viola because such accents are most often matters of melodic emphasis and the cello is usually concerned with non-melodic matters. The double bass is even less often called upon to sound chords for several reasons: the bulk of the instrument limits their availability, chords are generally ineffective in such a low register, and double basses are given a melodic role even less often than the cellos.

One more aspect of string playing remains; the use of the harmonic series. Referring again to Example 9, if the player places a finger lightly, so the string is not completely stopped, on the string at the point where A above middle C would normally be produced, bowing will produce the A one octave higher. This is called a *natural harmonic,* and is a result of the player's finger being on one of the nodes of harmonic number 3.

Natural harmonics are those produced by an open string. Harmonics numbered 2, 3, 4, 5, and 6 are available, but the last of these is not used because it is usually available as harmonic number 4 on a higher pitched string.

If the fundamental string length is obtained by stopping, the flexibility of the fingers is restricted. The player cannot stop the string and at the same time conveniently reach the various nodes. In such cases only the fourth harmonic is considered available. Again referring to the D string, Example 9, the tone F, three leger lines above the treble clef, may be sounded as a harmonic as follows: the player fully stops the string at the point indicated for F above middle C and simultaneously lightly stops the string at the point indicated for the B♭ above. This is called an *artificial harmonic.*

These natural and artificial harmonics are much more transparent, thin in quality and weaker in volume, than the ordinary string sound and are used only rarely. Orchestral players, however, occasionally use harmonics instead of ordinary tones when the fingering required for the ordinary tone is awkward or difficult. The universally recognized notation for them is a small zero above the tone to be produced as a harmonic, but many writers use more elaborate methods of notation in string music. The example below shows various ways to indicate that A, one leger line above the treble clef, is to be produced as a harmonic (sometimes called *"flageolet tone"*) on the violin.

The zero (a), is the simplest. (b) shows the open string, D; the point at which it is partially stopped, A; and the harmonic which results. In (c) the stopping place and the harmonic are shown. The string and the stopping place are shown in (d), and the harmonic is an inevitable result. An artificial harmonic is indicated in (e), and the player stops A on the fourth string with his first finger and partially stops D with his fourth finger. The high A results. The word "harmonic," (f), or "to be produced as harmonics," instructing the players to produce all tones as harmonics until further notice, is surprisingly little used. "Natural tones" or simply "natural" are the terms used to discontinue the harmonics. The diamond shaped note heads are used to indicate the point at which the string is partially stopped.

Although the harp to all outward appearances is a stringed instrument, its way of musical life is utterly foreign to all its orchestral colleagues. The harpist always arrives early, for his instrument must be tuned before every performance, just as the violin or ukulele—but one difference is that the harp has forty-seven strings. C♭ major can hardly be called a popular key, but that is the key to which the harp is tuned. There are seven strings to each octave, and the first is tuned to C♭, the second to D♭, and so on, until the scale is complete through six-and-one-half octaves. Other pitches are available through the use of a pedal mechanism that can be used to raise the pitch to its ♮ or ♯ condition. There is one pedal for each letter name: the C pedal controls every C string on the instrument, the D pedal controls every D, and so on. The D, C, and B pedals are situated at the base of the instrument where the player can get at them with his left foot. E, F, G, and A are at the base on the right. When a pedal is in its highest position, all the strings under its control sound the flat form of the letter —as in the C♭ major scale. If the pedal is lowered to its first notch, where it can be locked, it will cause all the pitches of its letter to sound natural. The second notch changes them all to sharps. For this reason, accidentals do not mean to the harpist what they mean to the rest of us. To him they mean pedaling.

Chromaticism is thus foreign to the harpist's nature; for since one string is responsible for three pitches, the following passage:

EXAMPLE 13

is playable only as G♯, A♮, B♭, C♭, B♯. The position of the pedal can be changed only when each of the strings controlled by it is unengaged. In the foregoing example the B♭ cannot be played as A♯, because the A string is sounded as A♮ and there is no time to pedal. B♮ must be played as C♭ because the B string immediately precedes it as B♭. This leaves no alternative but to play C as B♯ on the B string. If this were an isolated passage, it would pose no problem for the harpist, for he would prepare the pedals in advance to sound G♯, A♮, B♭, and C♭. When the fourth beat is reached, his left foot would depress the B pedal (which is in its flat position) to the second notch, B♯. It would then be ready for the following first beat.

If the passage were not preceded and followed by rests, there might be some difficulty, for the harp at the finish of this passage is tuned to G♯, A, B♯, and C♭; the D, E, and F strings have not been used and may be in any position.

More native to the harp are arpeggiated chords (its Italian name is *arpa,* from which the word *arpeggio* is derived) and the *glissando.* Any scale can be had in *glissando,* and many chords are playable also. Advance tuning to C♯, D♭, E♮, F♭, G♮, A♯, and B♭, makes it possible for the player to play a glissando on the diminished seventh chord sounding C♯, E, G, B♭. Any chord that can include all seven strings may be treated the same way: B♮, C♭, D♯, E♭, F♯, G♭, A♮ sounding B, D♯, F♯, A; B♮, C♭, D♮, E♯, F♮ G♯, A♭ sounding B, D, F, A♭; C♯, D♭, E♯, F♮, G♯, A♭, B♮ sounding D♭, F, A♭, C♭ are three of those possible. Others appear to be unusable because they cannot include all seven strings but have been used anyway. No one seems to be disturbed when what should be a C-E-G triad includes D and A.

The little fingers are not used in harp playing, being considered too weak and too short. Harmonics are frequently used. The harpist lightly touches the string at the exact center of its length. Plucking then sounds the second harmonic, one octave above the unstopped string. Finding the center of the string is not as simple as it sounds, for each string is not only of a different length but may also be in any one of the three pedal positions which vary the length. The range of tone color is small, consisting of the usual harp sound, harmonics, and a slight variation of the usual harp sound obtained by plucking the strings at a point well below the center, called *prés de la table.*

Percussion instruments are those which are used to produce sounds by being struck together, by being hit with sticks or mallets, or by being shaken, rattled, scraped, or activated by any means other than bowing, blowing, or plucking. This definition includes all sound effects—from the cannons in Tchaikovsky's *1812 Overture* to imitated bird calls, which, come to think of it, are blown. Most percussion instruments are of indeterminate pitch; others, like the celesta, xylophone, glockenspiel, and orchestral bells, have built-in scales. Only the timpani has controllable pitch, and the timpanist is by far the most important and most frequently employed percussionist.

Classical composers used two timpani, almost invariably tuned to tonic and dominant, but the modern player is usually equipped with three, and sometimes four timpani. Tuning is now accomplished by a pedal mechanism that controls the degree of tension of the drum head. The head is subject to atmospheric conditions, however, and the timpanist must usually refine the tuning by hand after pedaling to the desired pitch. A variety of mallets are used, ranging from softly padded ones to bare wooden sticks. The choice of drumstick is usually left to the discretion of the player, but it is sometimes specified in the score.

It is hoped that this cursory description of the mechanics of orchestral sound will prompt the reader to investigate further. Even an attempt to present every detail of each instrument's performance would fill more than one volume. The student who studies scores, listens to them, and who seeks out and studies instrumentalists in action will learn far more about the personalities, idioms, and capabilities of orchestral instruments than any written description can convey.

STUDIES

1. Write the harmonic series on each of the seven available fundamentals of the F part of the double horn. Do the same for the Bb part. Extend the series to the sixteenth harmonic in the first (open) position of the F horn and to the twelfth harmonic in all others.

2. Indicate the tenor trombone slide positions for each tone of the following:

(This is not to be taken as ideal trombone writing. It is intended to show that even seemingly simple passages can require awkward slide motion. Such melodic trombone parts always require special attention.)

3. Which of the woodwind instruments (Nos. 5 to 15 in the table of Ranges and Notations pages, 11 to 14) can play each of the following passages?

4. Write all the natural harmonics obtainable on: (a) the A string of violin; (b) the G string of viola; (c) the D string of cello; (d) the G string of double bass.

5. Write the five lowest-pitched artificial harmonics obtainable on: (a) the G string of violin; (b) the D string of viola; (c) the A string of cello.

6. Indicate the pedal changes required in the following passage when the harpist has preset the instrument to C♯, D♮, E♮, F♯, G♯, A♭, B♭. Copy the phrase using enharmonic spellings as played.

4

Transposition
and the C *Clef*

*T*HE WORLD is full of people, reasonable in most other respects, who think that all music should be written in the treble and bass clefs at actual sounding pitch. A glance at piccolo and contra-bassoon parts written according to their principle will show the fallacy of this attitude at once.

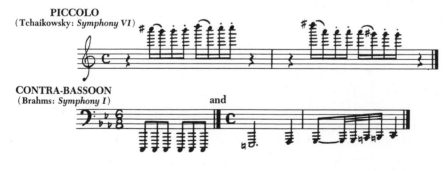

EXAMPLE 14

Both these instrumentalists, as well as all writers and readers of instrumental music are grateful for the fact that in this disagreeable world, agreement has been reached: piccolo music shall always be written one octave below the actual sound, and contra-bassoon music shall be written one octave above the actual sound, thereby bringing their notation into the realm of readability.

Octave transposition and the use of the C clef are the results of an aversion for leger lines and a similar aversion for clef changes. Other instruments which utilize the convenience of octave transposition are the double bass, celesta, xylophone, and guitar. The glockenspiel goes all out and sounds two octaves above the written pitch. An instance of octave transposition that results in inconvenience sometimes occurs in old cello music. Here, when the part ascends to the highest register, it is written in treble clef an octave above actual sound: there is no excuse for this custom, and it has long since been abandoned in instrumental music, but it remains in old scores to confuse the cellist.

Violas, violoncellos, bassoons, and tenor trombones frequently find themselves vacillating between the treble and bass clefs; for convenience, therefore, they use a suitable C clef. The C clef, 𝄡 , always indicates the location of middle C; the violas find it ideal for their range when, as an alto clef, it is situated on the middle line of the staff.

EXAMPLE 15

Cellos, bassoons, and first and second trombones sometimes find their parts lying so consistently above the bass clef that many leger lines are required. This is avoided through the employment of the C clef on the fourth line of the staff, that is, the tenor clef.

EXAMPLE 16

The alto and tenor clefs may be considered as combinations of the treble and bass clefs, for the alto clef encompasses the two lower lines of the treble clef, the middle C leger line, and the two upper lines of the

36

bass clef. The tenor clef uses only the lower line of the treble clef, middle C, and the three upper lines of the bass clef.

EXAMPLE 17

Players of wind instruments have a different problem. Many woodwind and brass instruments are duplicated in larger or smaller sizes, and the length of the air column changes accordingly, thus changing the pitch.

No one ever began his musical study as a player of the E♭ clarinet or alto flute or any other secondary member of the family of woodwind instruments. Most transposing instruments are so constructed for the benefit of the players, and a short history of a clarinetist will, it is hoped, make the reason clear.

The young aspirant to musicianship who selects the clarinet as his instrument is, in America, invariably given a B♭ clarinet. He is taught the fingerings for the complete range, and it soon becomes easy for him to play the following series of tones. (The numbers under each tone represent the fingering for present purposes only and have no connection with actual practice.)

EXAMPLE 18

Somewhere in the course of his studies the young clarinetist learns that every tone he produces sounds a major second below the letter name by which he identifies it. (There once was a clarinet in C in general use, but it is now obsolete and only its fingering nomenclature remains. The B♭ and A clarinets replaced it because of their longer tubes and richer tone quality.) As his career advances, he acquires a clarinet in A, a clarinet in E♭, and a bass clarinet; and he finds that with slight changes of embouchure he can play them all, using the now ingrained technics of his early training. He finds that fingering 1, which he calls C, produces the

Bb below on the Bb clarinet, the A below on the A clarinet, the Eb above on the Eb clarinet and the Bb a ninth below on the bass clarinet. His fingered chromatic scale from C produces the following sounds on the various instruments:

EXAMPLE 19

As he plays in ensemble groups, he finds that the composer or orchestrator has written his parts according to this common fingering pattern. If he wants Eb from the Eb clarinet, he writes C; if he wants Ab from the Bb clarinet, he writes Bb; and so on, as given in the range and notation chart at the beginning of Chapter 2. This makes it possible for the clarinetist to use the same technic of fingering in playing the various sized clarinets.

If the parts given to him were written at actual pitch, he would be burdened with the following:

EXAMPLE 20

$$\left\{\begin{array}{l}\text{Eb on the Eb clarinet: fingering 1 (C).}\\ \text{Eb on the Bb clarinet: fingering 6 (F).}\\ \text{Eb on the A clarinet: fingering 7 (F}\sharp\text{).}\\ \text{Eb on the bass clarinet: fingering 18 (F).}\end{array}\right.$$

The situation would be similar to that of the experienced driver who might buy a sports car and find that what he thought was the steering wheel controls the brakes, and that the old familiar brake pedal controls the windshield wipers. Or, if he tried to drive a truck, he might discover that the steering wheel-brake control is now the accelerator, and the former brake pedal-windshield wiper control is now the light switch. Many traffic accidents have been avoided because the manufacturers of motor vehicles have agreed that the system of control should be consistent, not modified according to steering ratio, horsepower rating, and braking efficiency. And many orchestral accidents are likewise avoided because the writers of music long years ago learned that it is safer to arrange, in the solitude of their studios, the notation according to the convenience of the instrumentalist than to expect a performer to make these adjustments under the pressure of the concert hall.

Alto flute and English horn are also transposing instruments, for they are always played by flutists and oboists.

Brass instruments have historical precedents to justify their transposition.

The sound of the horn (known as the French horn in Britain and America, but not in France) has always been attractive to composers. Before valves were in use, composers devoted much effort to writing music which could be played on the hand horn, an instrument that had only one harmonic series and a few muffled hand-in-the-bell tones as its repertoire of pitches. The mastery with which they dealt with this limitation is worthy of more attention than it has received. Mendelssohn's *Midsummer Night's Dream Nocturne* is a good example of a piece written for hand horn.

The eighteenth- or early nineteenth-century horn player had, as his orchestral equipment, a circular tube resembling a denuded modern horn, and a collection of plumbing called "crooks." The crooks were sections of tubing of various lengths, made to fit into the tube of the horn. One crook or another was fitted to the tube as required, to increase its length and make available a new, lower pitched, harmonic series. To the horn player who used crooks, notation was the least important part of his problem, for the convenient convention of writing all horn music in the harmonic series of C was standard practice. This served a double purpose: the player was never bothered by a key signature, and he could tell at a glance which harmonic was required. A written middle C was always the fourth harmonic over the fundamental provided by the crook. The pitches written in these old horn parts were never intended to represent pitch; they represented only the harmonics:

EXAMPLE 21

39

The bass clef notation in the wrong octave in Example 21 is unexplainable, except perhaps that it may have been used to emphasize the lowness of the pitch. Or, it may be a reflection of the old cello treble clef notation, where high pitches were written an octave too high. Horn parts when written in bass clef were, and unfortunately in some cases still are, written below the actual sound rather than above. Confusion can be avoided by restricting horn parts to the treble clef, using leger lines when necessary.

This written series of harmonics, with an occasional B♮, E♭, C♯, A, high F♮, or low F♯, was the material from which horn music was made until valves made the chromatic scale available throughout the compass. The old valveless instrument is sometimes referred to as the hand horn, for the out-of-tune tones of the natural harmonic series could be corrected, and a few other tones added to the repertoire by manipulation of the right hand in the bell of the instrument. These so called "stopped tones" were rather muffled in quality, and composers took pains to avoid requiring that they be accented. The hand in the bell is still an important part of the horn player's technic and is the principal reason for the unique position in which the instrument is held. The bell is turned away from the audience in order to make it accessible to the player's right hand. As a consequence the horn is the only brass instrument whose valves are controlled by the left hand. The series was available in most keys and always sounded lower than the written C series as follows:

Horn in B♭ alto sounded a major second below the written pitch.
Horn in A sounded a minor third below the written pitch.
Horn in G sounded a perfect fourth below the written pitch.
Horn in F sounded a perfect fifth below the written pitch.
Horn in E sounded a minor sixth below the written pitch.
Horn in E♭ sounded a major sixth below the written pitch.
Horn in D sounded a minor seventh below the written pitch.
Horn in C sounded an octave below the written pitch.
Horn in B♭ sounded a major ninth below the written pitch.

Crooks for other pitches were made and used, but these are the most usual.

Early trumpeters used crooks also, but not as many as horn players. The harmonic series of C was used in trumpet notation also, but the tones sometimes sounded higher than the written pitch:

Trumpet in C sounds as written.
Trumpet in B♭ sounds a major second below written pitch.

Trumpet in A sounds a minor third below written pitch.
Trumpet in F sounds a perfect fourth above written pitch.
Trumpet in E sounds a major third above written pitch.
Trumpet in Eb sounds a minor third above written pitch.
Trumpet in D sounds a major second above written pitch.

The trombone, because it has always been able to change the fundamental and to sound any desired pitch, and the tuba, because it is a relatively recent addition to the orchestra (nineteenth century, after the crooking damage had been done), have never been troubled with transposition.

One other notation device remains to be considered. In many old scores there arc timpani parts that include only C and G. This notation represents the tonic and dominant of the key (the tonic was always specified on the first page of the score), for the timpanist invariably tuned his larger drum to the dominant and his smaller drum to the tonic. He hit the big one when G was specified and the smaller one when C appeared in his part. The probable reason for this notation is that when the timpani was played, the trumpets and horns were usually played also. Since these brass parts were always notated in C, and the horns, trumpets, and timpani were grouped together in the score, it was probably thought best to write them all in the same key.

Transposition as it occurs in modern scores is given above in the range and notation chart, pp. 9-19. Old scores usually include parts for brass instruments crooked in keys other than those now most commonly used. All these transpositions must be mastered by anybody who hopes to understand orchestral music.

Instantaneous transposition may be accomplished through the use of clefs, for there are enough clefs to locate middle C on any line of the staff.

EXAMPLE 22

It has been shown that the alto and tenor clefs are made up of various lines of the more familiar treble and bass clefs; the other clefs may be similarly approached.

41

SOPRANO

MEZZO SOPRANO

BARITONE

EXAMPLE 23

A part for horn in E, written

EXAMPLE 24

may be read with an imaginary bass clef and key signature of four sharps to reveal the sounding pitch one octave too low:

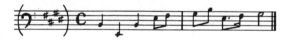

EXAMPLE 25

If the same passage is written for horn in D, the actual sounding pitch names are seen when the alto clef with a two-sharp key signature is used:

EXAMPLE 26

If the same passage is marked horn in B♭, and a player using a modern horn in F were to play it, he could apply the mezzo-soprano clef and obtain the correct result as follows:

1. Written notation in C as in Example 24.

2. Sound on B♭ horn.

EXAMPLE 27

3. Notation for F horn.

EXAMPLE 28

4. Original notation as read by the player.

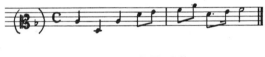

EXAMPLE 29

By using the various clefs in this manner, any transposed part may be restored to actual pitch or placed in any desired key. Sometimes the result will be an octave too low or too high, but the correct adjustment is easily made.

It is traditional to write horn parts without key signatures and to indicate accidentals as they occur. One reason for this is, of course, the C-major history of the instrument. Another is the danger that, while dealing with a transposition such as the one just discussed, the player might forget which of the three keys involved (C, F, and B♭ in this instance) is actually in effect. The tradition is being abandoned, however, and most contemporary horn players advocate the use of key signatures. Since all horn parts are now written for the F horn, there is no longer any reason to treat it differently from the other transposing instruments.

Orderly and efficient as clef transposition is, it is not in general use among instrumentalists. Trumpet and horn players, and, to a lesser extent, clarinetists are the few players who are accustomed to reading music in a key that is not the key of their instrument. Most of them simply calculate the interval between the written part and the instrument they are playing and transpose at that interval. For example, a trumpet player with a B♭ instrument in his hands and a part for trumpet in D on the stand before him realizes that the interval between B♭ and D is a major third, and he merely plays every written note a major third above.

EXAMPLE 30

Although the bass clef would give the correct pitch names, it may be distracting to the player because of its association with low pitches. The player's transposition problem runs a poor second to his concern about playing high-register parts written for a small trumpet on a larger trumpet, where the high tones are much more difficult.

The horn player has similar problems. His parts appear in a greater multiplicity of keys and require a greater range of tones.

The following passage:

EXAMPLE 31

written for a B♭ horn sounds

EXAMPLE 32

but the same notes written for a horn in G sound

EXAMPLE 33

44

Both these and all other horn keys are now played on the double horn in F and B♭, but it is important that the player know the composer's original designation of the instrument to be used. The quality of tone emitted by old high horns differs from that of low horns; and although the composer's choice of horn key may have been governed by necessity or convenience more than by his preference for a particular tone color, it still behooves the player to consider both possibilities.

Transposition by interval requires that the player keep the interval constantly in mind with a consequent consciousness of the relative height or depth of the originally notated part. In any case, the old trumpet and horn parts are not difficult to transpose, for they were largely limited to the tones of the harmonic series. A passage such as:

HORN I in D
(Haydn: *Oxford Symphony*)

EXAMPLE 34

may be easily read if it is borne in mind that C always represents the tonic, G its dominant, and E the major third.

Clarinet parts are written in B♭, A, C, D, and E♭. Those who play the B♭, A, and C parts are equipped with a pair of instruments pitched in B♭ and A, and they have only a major second or a minor third transposition to deal with. Invariably, when clarinetists play a C clarinet part, they use the instrument (B♭ or A) on which the written C part "lies best," and transpose by interval without undue strain. D clarinet music is now always played on the little E♭ clarinet, and the transposition requires only a change of key signature. This frequently causes very awkward situations for the player, and clef transposition would not help him execute a passage written for D clarinet in the key of G on an E♭ clarinet in the key of G♭.

The orchestrator is obliged to familiarize himself with these matters because they are an integral part of the orchestral technic. Fluent score-reading requires a sound technic of transposition, and almost any scoring task is made more difficult if facility in transposition is lacking.

STUDIES

1. Write the following for E♭ clarinet, clarinet in A, bass clarinet (French notation), bassoon (use the tenor clef), horn in F, B♭ trumpet, and viola. Each should sound in unison with the given melody, not an octave above or below.

2. Transpose the following: (a) to the actual sounding key, using two staves, with treble and bass clefs; (b) for four horns in F, using two staves, with treble clefs.

3. Rewrite the following melody

(a) in the alto clef;
(b) in the tenor clef;
(c) in the soprano clef.
(d) Which clef would be used to place this passage in the proper key for Eb clarinet? Copy the passage given, and substitute the clef, adjust the accidentals, and indicate any required octave transposition.
(e) Which clef would be used to place this passage in the proper key for Bb clarinet? Follow the same procedure as in (d) above.
(f) Which clef would be used to place this passage in the proper key for horn in F? Follow the same procedure as in (d) above.
(g) Which clef would be used to place this passage in the proper key for clarinet in A? Follow the same procedure as in (d) above.

5

The Orchestral Score

EACH AND EVERY STUDENT of orchestration, composition, and conducting is able, at small cost, to obtain accurate orchestral scores of the works of every major (and, it sometimes seems every minor) contributor to the literature. Miniature scores (such as those on page 000 and 000) are invaluable to teachers, students, and literate music lovers. They are not, however, suitable for the use of working conductors, nor are they fitting models for the orchestrator. The conductor's score must be one that shows at a glance what the composer wants from each instrument. Miniature scores, planned as study scores, usually include on each score page only those instruments that happen to take part in the measures that can be fitted onto it. Any instrumental part may appear on the top or any other line, or two or more score pages may appear on a single page. This requires the reader to pay almost as much attention to the marginal indications (who is where) as he devotes to the music.

The conductor, busy as he is, has no time for this; he requires a score with one entire score page per page, in which the instruments are always in the same relative positions.

The orchestrator may conceive of his scoring plan in one minute; but since he must then spend many times that amount of time writing the plan down, he has a different viewpoint. He is interested in shortcuts in notation.

Hence, there are three types of scores in use: the miniature score, for study; the conductor's score, for practical use; and the manuscript score, for convenience in notation.

The conductor's score and the manuscript score do not differ very much. Any conductor can, and regularly does, give public performances using unpublished manuscript scores.

One page of a printed conductor's score, a reproduction of page 102 of the Breitkopf and Härtel edition of Beethoven's Ninth Symphony, is reproduced below side by side with a manuscript copy of the same excerpt as it might be notated by a present-day orchestrator. It is reduced in size, for the size of the actual score is 10 by 13 inches. The paper on which the manuscript copy is written is 9½ by 11½ inches.

The scores do not name the instruments. These were indicated on the first page of the movement, and the line assigned to them there is maintained throughout, until another arrangement is given. An experienced conductor would have no difficulty in identifying the instrumental parts, for the brackets and the key signatures indicate each group of participants.

The manuscript score uses the following shortcuts:

1. Instead of writing out repeated measures and pairs of measures, the symbol •/. is used. If the symbol is contained within a single measure the preceding measure is repeated. If it is spread over two measures the two preceding measures are repeated.

2. Full-measure rests are omitted. Any measure that contains one or more notes that do not add up to the number of beats of a full measure is completed with rests.

3. Parts which duplicate each other in every detail are written in only one part, and the word *Colla* or its abbreviation *Col* is written for the duplicating instruments. The instrument for which the part is written is also designated. Lines 2 and 12 of the manuscript score are examples.

4. First and second flutes, oboes, clarinets, and bassoons are paired on one line each. This is possible only where the two parts can be clearly indicated on one line, as they are in this example. Usually, however, whole movements must be considered by the orchestrator, not only one page, as here.

The line above the first violin is often left blank because the space is needed for tempo indications. The omission also isolates the strings, and makes it easier to read.

EXAMPLE 35

EXAMPLE 36

51

As we compare the two pages line by line, the differences between the formal printed conductor's score and the hastily written manuscript score become obvious. The line numbers used in the following discussion refer to the printed score; and after the instruments are named, all comments refer to the manuscript version.

Lines 1 and 2: first and second flutes, combined on one line.

Lines 3 and 4: first and second oboes, combined on one line. *1* indicates that only the first oboe plays; at *a 2* in measure 7, second oboe joins first oboe at the unison.

Lines 5 and 6: first and second clarinets in C. C clarinets are now obsolete and in the manuscript score the parts are transposed. If C clarinets were used, the part would not have been written out, and the indication *Col Fl. II* would have been used instead, as in the oboe parts. The two parts are, as flutes and oboes, written on one line.

Lines 7 and 8: first and second bassoons. Again the two are combined on one line.

Lines 9 and 10: line 9 is for first and second horns in D, and line 10 for third and fourth horns in B♭. All parts are written for horns in F in modern scores, and although the manuscript score is a faithful copy, a modern orchestrator feels a strong temptation to add to the second and third parts. The B♭ horns would surely have been given more than three notes if Beethoven had had the modern instruments available.

Line 11: first and second trumpets in D. Here again the limitation of classical brasses is shown. B♭ trumpets are used because they are most frequently available, but C trumpets could have been used instead. Either would contribute to this *tutti* passage far more richly than the old tonic-dominant crooked trumpets.

Line 12: timpani, placed below the two trombone lines. The octave F–F tuning was an innovation in its day. Apparently Beethoven was the first to tune the drums to anything other than tonic and dominant.

Lines 13 and 14: trombones. They are used remarkably little in this movement, but their place in the score is reserved. Their location, below the timpani, in the printed score is an archaism and is a manifestation of the musical experimentation of the nineteenth century.

Lines 15 and 16: first and second violins. The tempo indications above the first violin are necessary, for this is where the conductor's eyes are usually focused.

Line 17: violas. Reproduced exactly.

Lines 18 and 19: violoncellos and double basses, combined on one line. No *a 2* or *unis* indication is required, for these two are combined more often than not.

The manuscript score shows the instruments in the up-to-down order that is now standard usage.

The now commonly used pattern is a fairly recent development, and nineteenth century scores show a considerable diversity of practice. First and second violins and violas were for some years assigned the upper three lines. Trombones appear below timpani in Beethoven's Ninth Symphony score, and the vocal parts in the Finale are inserted between violas and cellos. Wagner's operas were published with the trombones below the trumpets, where they logically belong; but all the vocal and dramatic proceedings are still among the string parts, as in Beethoven's scores.

The first page of each score shows the instrumentation and the relative position of all participants. These positions are maintained throughout the movement, and when instruments are added or deleted for other movements, another "first score page" shows the new arrangement.

A summary of current and recommended manuscript scoring procedure is given in Chapter 7.

Mention of nontransposed scores may be in order here. Recently there has been some interest in writing full orchestral scores to show each instrumental part (except those which transpose an octave) as it sounds, rather than as it appears to the players. There are good reasons for the lack of success of this plan. First, those whose business it is to use scores are usually so well versed in the workings of instruments that an English horn part that descends two or more leger lines below the treble clef unnerves them. Horn parts that eternally hover around the lower half of the treble clef and usually fit better into the bass clef just do not look like horn parts. Clarinetists of the eighteenth and nineteenth century were never required to face key signatures with more than a few accidentals; and their contemporaries who played the trumpet spent their lives playing a few C's and G's, one each of D and F, and very little else. When parts for these instruments appear in a score at actual pitch, identification with the truth of performance is lost, and the experienced score-reader's perspective is destroyed.

The key signatures of the transposing instruments serve as guideposts on each score page and help to identify instruments in conductors' scores. This advantage too is lost when the key signature is the same for all instruments. Perhaps the truth of the matter is that untransposed scores are designed for amateurs who are unable to read a real score; and because few amateurs will admit that they require a patronizingly simplified version of orchestral music, these scores are not successful. Amateurs hate to be patronized!

6

$\mathcal{N}$otation

$\mathcal{I}$N ORDER TO bring to life the music of both the past and present, the vagaries of musical notation in the literature as it has been left to us must be understood by all performers. Carefully controlled nuance and articulation are a part of every modern performance, but these are the result of the skill, experience, and intuitive musicianship of the players and the conductor more often than they are the inevitable result of an accurate reading of the score.

Instrumental notation of the baroque and early classical periods shows little more than pitch, rhythm, and meter. Tempo and dynamic indications are often lacking.

Composers of the later classical era were slightly more concerned with the problems of the performer and were usually careful to indicate the bowing of the string parts. Woodwind players, however, were given parts in which the phrasing and articulations were written as though they were to be bowed, and each woodwind instrumentalist was and is obliged to adapt the bowing instructions to the individual tongueing and breathing requirements of his instrument. Brass players were rarely given more than a slur over two or three notes to help them perform in conformity with the ensemble.

The nineteenth century saw the advent of the orchestral concert; and composers, who could hardly escape or ignore the tribulations of rehearsal, apparently were sufficiently impressed to try to be more exact in their scores.

Examine the scores in Part Two in chronological order (Schubert, Mendelssohn, Tchaikovsky, Grieg, Debussy, Ravel) with reference to the notation of phrasing, bowing, and dynamic indications. Notice how the variety and frequency of markings increases and how the wind parts are given more individual attention as the modern era is approached. If scores of the eighteenth century were to be similarly surveyed, the beginnings of interpretive notation would be seen.

In addition to the differences between periods, the orchestra must cope with inadequately written scores, the results of careless and indifferent or inconsistent notation of all eras.

This lyric flute solo

(Bach: *St. Matthew Passion*)

EXAMPLE 37

is written in typical baroque style. The last two measures of the example could be articulated as the slurs (or are they bowing indications?) imply, but surely each tone in the first two measures (except the two to which the appoggiaturas are attached) is not to be given an individually tongued articulation!

A more modern flute solo shows more clearly the articulation intended, but when is the player to take a breath?

(Grieg: *Piano Concerto*)

EXAMPLE 38

55

Orchestral instrumentalists are required to edit the phrasing of many standard and familiar works, for neither of the two preceding illustrations can be effectively performed as written. Nor are these isolated examples; almost any pre-1900 score—and too many modern ones—involve similar problems for the players.

The string literature requires as much revision as the woodwind repertoire. Both quotations in Example 39 would be questioned by any string player, for the first seems to call for a bow-stroke on each tone, and the second indicates that the whole passage is to be played on only one stroke of the bow. The bow would probably have to be at least four feet in length to produce a reasonably full tone throughout the phrase!

EXAMPLE 39

In Scarlatti's day violinists were quite likely to bow each tone, but modern players, with their more brilliant-toned instruments, can be subtle. In Example 39 Wagner probably meant to show phrasing, not bowing. He was not very consistent about it, but many modern string players recommend this practice of writing phrasing instead of bowing. No matter how exact and reasonable the written bowing may be, it is the concertmaster or the conductor who is the final authority; and even the most familiar and often played orchestral compositions are likely to be bowed differently by different orchestras. Common sense therefore dictates that it is wisest to phrase rather than bow, but by doing so the orchestrator surrenders an important means of communication with the players. The first concern of the orchestra is the realization of the composer's ideas. If, in order to attain this end, a revision of bowing is considered necessary, the composer or orchestrator may be grateful that such revisions are undertaken by experts: artists whose only purpose is effective performance.

Woodwind and brass music may be written with unmistakably specific indications of articulation and breathing places; but, in the minds of most composers, wind instrumentalists are secondary to the strings, and when a woodwind instrument doubles a string part, its notation, as was once the universal practice, duplicates the bowing. The wind player is well aware of the technics of interpretation and will devote his efforts to the consummation of the musical thought through good ensemble. The point of all this is not to prove that Bach, Scarlatti, Grieg, and Wagner did not know how to write music, but to show that every orchestral player is equipped and quite ready to modify the phrasing or bowing of any passage that seems to him to need revision.

The orchestrator must prepare his scores with all possible clarity of detail; he then may rest assured that his work will be sympathetically dealt with by those whose profession it is to bring inanimate pages of notes to life.

In addition to the need to be clear about phrasing, the orchestrator must accurately indicate dynamics and must consider the instruments that neither bow nor blow their tones into existence.

Nuance, which is largely a matter of the degree of emphasis or de-emphasis of individual tones, is represented in scores by crescendo and decrescendo signs and a variety of dynamic indications, *ppp* to *fff*. It is important that these symbols be liberally dispersed, but a word of warning is of value here. All orchestral instrumentalists are ensemble players and will fit their tones to the ensemble rather than observe an arbitrary conception of *forte* or *piano*. All dynamic markings are relative to the musical situation, that which follows and that which precedes. Dynamic markings are too often a general indication of what the orchestrator would like to hear rather than what they will mean to the players. No error in orchestral balance has ever been corrected by a *p* in the overweighted instruments and an *f* in the underweighted ones. It is the conductor's function to establish and control the balance between instruments; the dynamic indications in the parts are little more than generalizations.

Percussion instruments and the harp are without any semblance of a legato, and there is no point in indicating phrasing in their music.

Harp music is usually written in accordance with the common practice of harmonic and melodic notation. Since there is frequently more than one way to pedal a given passage, and players may not always agree about which is best, it is probably unwise for the orchestrator to intrude. This policy is abandoned when a glissando is required. It is customary to indicate the tuning of the seven letters and add the word *glissando*. Having given the tuning and the method of performance, it remains only to indicate the extent of the *glissando* and its metrical location. In the example below, the harpist is shown the tuning of each string (which he has prepared during the preceding silent measures), and he gauges the speed of the glissando to the tempo, for the glissando must be timed to arrive at the high F on the first beat of the second measure. (*Etouffez* after the high F directs the player to stop the tone at once, that is, not to let it ring, as is natural to the instrument.)

HARP I
(Ravel: *Daphne et Chloe,*
Suite No. 2)

EXAMPLE 40

It is pointless to write all the tones included in the *glissando,* for besides being tedious to set down, they would serve no purpose. The pedals cannot be changed, and only octave duplications of the prearranged tuning can be had.

The players of percussion instruments, are probably the most frequent victims of careless notation. The fundamental characteristic of stick technic can be quickly grasped if a pencil or similar substitute for a drumstick is taken in each hand and the following rhythms tapped out with alternating left- and right-hand strokes:

EXAMPLE 41

Notice that the rhythm of the first two or three measures can be clearly understood; but as the speed of reiteration increases, the exact division of strokes within the meter becomes less obvious to the ear. As this identifiable rhythmic function of the strokes becomes obscured, the impulse toward an accent becomes stronger, and a point is reached where the last stroke is heard as an accent even though it may occur on the smallest fractional division of a weak beat. Neglect of this aspect of drumming is common, and percussionists know that they must usually adjust their performance to the situation at hand rather than depend upon the written part. Two examples may serve to illustrate:

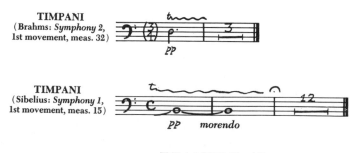

TIMPANI
(Brahms: *Symphony 2,*
1st movement, meas. 32)

TIMPANI
(Sibelius: *Symphony 1,*
1st movement, meas. 15)

EXAMPLE 42

In the first quotation the timpanist is a soloist. Trombones and tuba enter softly on the first beat of the measure following the timpani *tremolando*. The Sibelius example, which shows the last two measures of a sixteen-measure roll, accompanies a clarinet solo that pauses with the timpani at the end of measure 17.

In neither of these passages is an accent permissible at the end of the roll. In the Brahms, the timpanist must decide upon one of three alternatives. The roll may be carried over the bar line and the last stroke made on the first beat of measure 33 where it will be covered by the low brass. It should then have been written

EXAMPLE 43

The second alternative is to continue the roll to the fraction of a second preceding the bar line. This is what the written part seems to require, but it is most unnatural to the instrument, for the tendency of final strokes to sound accented must somehow be overcome.

A less probable, but quite possible, decision might be to end the roll on the accented beat closest to the end of the measure. Accented beats, in this sense and usage, are those parts of beats or pulses which retain their identity in experiments such as that in Example 41. Although a skilled percussionist controls the action of his mallets more expeditiously than the pencil-equipped novice, the line of separation between recognizable accents and strokes that require a subsequent accent can be easily found by all who take the trouble to search.

If this third alternative is used, the part would be written:

EXAMPLE 44

This third alternative is also the logical choice for the Sibelius example, for the fermata over the bar line prohibits any sound there. The music permits no accent before this pause, or, more exactly, no syncopation: that is, displacement of accent. Syncopation always conveys a feeling of urgency, which is uncalled for here; and the timpanist must guard against the slightest hint of it. He must either make a diminuendo that

59

disappears at the instant before the fermata or end his roll on a secondary pulsation similar to the third alternative in Example 43. This use of secondary accents is important to percussionists, for the final stroke loses its accent when it is concurrent with a pulsation that is unanimously felt by the whole ensemble.

It should now be understood that the object of notation is to give the conductor and the instrumentalists the clearest possible written representation of the composer's or orchestrator's intention.

Bowing or phrasing may be used for string instruments; the choice must be left to the individual writer. If phrasing is used, it is well to say so at the beginning of each part. Otherwise the players might decide that the orchestrator is an ignoramus whose writing is not to be taken seriously. The composer or copyist should make certain that parts for wind instruments show breathing places and incidental articulations, and harp and percussion parts are written according to the requirements of their method of performance.

Clarity, neatness, and good spacing are essential. All dynamics and phrasings must be consistent throughout the orchestra, for if a dynamic marking is omitted in one part, the player and conductor may conclude that a special effect is being sought. It is considerate, when making instrumental parts, to arrange things so a rest appears at the bottom of pages to be turned.

Very few instrumentalists enjoy playing from manuscript music, and if the manuscript part is poorly done or contains many ambiguities or inaccuracies, the players' faith in the writer is shaken and an indifferent performance may be the result. It is not difficult to understand the players' firm belief that someone who doesn't know how to write orchestral parts doesn't know how to orchestrate.

7

A Guide to Preparing the Orchestral Score in Manuscript

A. The order of instruments, from top down, is normally as follows: piccolo, flutes, oboes, English horn, Eb clarinet, Bb or A clarinets, bass clarinet, bassoons, contra-bassoon, horns, trumpets, trombones, tuba, timpani, percussion, harp, first violins, second violins, violas, cellos, double basses.

Vocal or solo instrumental parts appear below the harp and above first violin.

B. Clefs and key signatures appear on every line and every page. The time signature appears at the beginning of each part and wherever changes occur. Manuscript score paper with instruments and clefs already printed on it is available. It is recommended, for it saves most of the labor of these first two steps.

C. Dynamics and phrasing indications appear in every part.

D. Tempo indications appear above the top line and above the first violin.

E. Bar lines are continuous from the top line through all parts down to the bass.

F. In manuscript scores it is common practice to omit all full-measure rests. If the measure contains less than a full measure of notes, it must be completed with rests; but if it contains no notes, it is left blank because it is too tedious to write the rests in. Besides, full-measure rests are frequently a hindrance to score reading, for they are likely to be more eye-catching than the parts for the performing instruments.

G. When two or more instruments of the same group are doubled at the same pitch for any considerable length of time, the part may be written only once. For instance, for doubled first and second violins, write the part for first violin. On the second violin line write *Col. Vln. I*, and in each measure thereafter draw a diagonal dash, */*, to indicate that the doubling is still in effect.

This abbreviation may *not* be used:

1. For instruments of different groups, such as flute and violin, because the bowing marks for violin and the phrasing for flute are not the same.

2. For instruments of different pitch, such as oboe and clarinet. The clarinet part must be transposed.

3. For instruments using different clefs, such as violin, viola, and cello.

H. When a measure is repeated exactly, the symbol */. in the second measure may replace the repetition. If two measures are repeated, the sign is spread over the two measures in which the repetition takes place.

I. Two woodwind or brass parts or two parts for a divided string section may be written on the same line: first and second flute, bass trombone and tuba, and so on.

The parts for each must be clearly indicated. Common usage is as follows:

1. First and second in unison: one part marked *a 2*.

2. First alone: *1*.

3. Second alone: *2*.

4. Separate parts: first part stems up, second part stems down.

5. Divided strings: as above, marked *divisi*. If this indication is omitted the players will assume that double-stopping is intended. When the divided section ends the part should be marked *Tutti*.

6. Be consistent within each phrase in the use of terminology; that is, use only *a 2*, or use the stem system.

If the two parts are complex and unlike each other, separate lines may be used.

J. The parts in the score should, except for the abbreviations described above, be written as they will ultimately appear to the player. For example, do not use the term *8va* to avoid leger lines, for problems of execution are very different in the upper registers of most instruments.

K. Care should be taken to space the parts correctly, vertically as well as horizontally.

L. Rehearsal Marks: If the score is to be performed, it is important that rehearsal marks be included in order to facilitate the inevitable stops and starts during the preparation for performance. Letters, numbers, or measure numbers may be used, and should be spaced not too far apart.

STUDIES

1. Copy the last six measures of Tchaikovsky's *Danse russe Trepak,* page 174. Use all allowable abbreviations as described in this chapter.

2. The following is a reduction of an excerpt from Béla Bartók's Concerto for Orchestra. Score it as directed below, using abbreviations.

Line 1: second violin, first oboe, first Bb clarinet. Doubled in the octave above for first violin, first and second flutes. Piccolo is written in the same octave as the flutes and sounds another octave above.

Line 2: second oboe, second Bb clarinet. Doubled in the octave below in first and second bassoons and cello. Use the tenor clef for these three parts.

Line 3: third oboe, third Bb clarinet, viola.

Line 4: first and second trumpets in C.

Line 5: first and third horns in F.

Line 6: second and fourth horns in F.

Line 7: third bassoon, third trombone, tuba. Doubled in the octave above in first trombone (tenor clef). Double bass is written in the same octave as first trombone and sounds in unison with the third bassoon, third trombone, and tuba.

63

Second trombone, first and second harps, timpani and percussion, used elsewhere in the score, do not take part in this passage. The third oboist, the third clarinetist, and the third bassoonist may, in other sections of the work, be called upon to play English horn, bass clarinet, and contra-bassoon, respectively, with the piccolo player doubling on the third flute part.

3. Analyze the following melody. Copy it, adding: (a) bowing, as for violin; (b) the natural phrasing, with slurs from one breathing place to the next, as for a wind instrument; (c) articulations within the phrases, as for a wind instrument.

8

The Orchestral Role of Instruments

THE ORCHESTRA IS the most flexible and varied medium of expression available to the composer. The study of orchestration must include the study of compositional technics and textures, for no combination of instruments can be classified as effective or ineffective until considered in the light of its musical context. Any orchestral instrument may be combined with any other or combination of others if justified by the musical situation, and there is no hard and fast rule of instrumentation which applies to every circumstance. The only guides to effectiveness are stylistic consistency, idiomatic instrumental usage, and indefinable musical instinct. The concurrent maintenance of continuity and variety, absolutely essential as it is, must in large measure be a result of instinct, and style is sometimes an elusive element. Anyone can become familiar with instrumental technics, however, and it is probably for this reason that so many studies· called "Orchestration" are only manuals of instrumental capabilities and limitations.

The following discussion is based on the assumption that anyone who finds that the perusal of these words is unavoidable possesses a musical instinct that will see him through. Illustrations of interesting aspects of orchestral usage appear in every orchestral score; but since fragmentary quotations are unavoidably quotations out of context, none will be included here, and the reader is referred to the library, the concert hall, and the listening booth. The illustrations included were invented by the author to clarify certain technics, and are not parts of any score.

THE STRINGS

The strings *are* the orchestra. An old generalization holds that the woodwinds are added for color, the brass for power, and the percussion for rhythm. The string orchestra possesses each of these qualities to a degree sufficient for the expression of a great many musical ideas, and there exists a large repertoire of music for strings alone.

The strings bring to the symphonic ensemble all their individual and diversified tone qualities, an almost unlimited technical facility, and an ability to combine with all other instruments in every role running from soloist to least competitive accompanist. Their tone quality can be varied from rich to bland. They seldom appear alone; but they are a constant orchestral factor and are by far the most consistently conspicuous.

The fundamental conception of the string section, which was in effect during the orchestra's early adolescence but still remains valid, relates the instruments to the equivalent human voices. First violin is soprano, second violin is alto, viola is tenor, and violoncello is bass. Double basses are so named because of their function: they double the bass in the lower octave when additional strength or depth is needed or desired.

It may be mentioned here that the French term for viola is "alto." This unfortunate circumstance should not be permitted to lead the novice astray, for French scores also assign the tenor part to these altos. There is logic in the French terminology, for if the violin is soprano, the next lower-pitched instrument must be alto; but it should be understood that it is not, like the double bass, named for its normal orchestral function.

Many pages of the standard literature show the strings in this arrangement, often with one or two parts doubled in a woodwind, or with a woodwind and horn combination as background. Choral equivalents are not always adhered to; and frequently the texture becomes first violin, melody; cello-double bass, bass; and second violin and viola inner accompaniment. Even so, the basic conception remains.

Another frequently encountered distribution, more common in modern scores and usually requiring the participation of winds, is the assignment of first and second violins in octaves to a melodic passage. The role of cello and double bass is unchanged, but violas are left alone to cope with both or either of the alto and tenor parts. In this situation the violas may play a composite of the two inner parts, one or the other of them; or the orchestrator may avoid the problem entirely and double the second violin. In each of these cases winds are required to assist, for octave-doubled first and second violins, and octave-doubled cello and double bass are heavy opposition for divided or undivided violas.

When the strings are called upon to play only three parts—as in a three-voice harmonic or contrapuntal structure, for instance, or as the three accompanying parts to a melodic upper voice in woodwinds—either the violas or second violins are rendered more or less superfluous. The classical masters, possibly because they were reluctant to omit any of the ordinarily none-too-plentiful strings, usually doubled violas with the cello bass line, in unison or at the octave above. Rests for unrequired strings are more common in recent scores.

Toward the end of the nineteenth century, another method of scoring for strings was developed. It is interesting to speculate as to whether this was the result of orchestral influence upon compositional technics or an example of the orchestra's ability to adapt itself to the composer's demands. The orchestral influence may have been due to the beautiful oneness of the string instruments. The compositional technic may have been the discovery[1] that melodies can be doubled not only at the octave, but at other intervals or combinations of intervals without implying individuality of line, but only reinforcing the principal melody.

At any rate it is now common practice to subdivide the upper strings. This simple passage

---

1. Or rediscovery. Organum of the ninth century anticipated the device, and it has not been wholly absent from the musical scene since.

which no orchestrator would hesitate to score

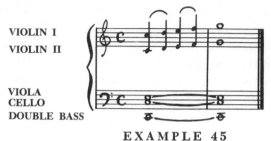

EXAMPLE 45

may also be scored as follows:

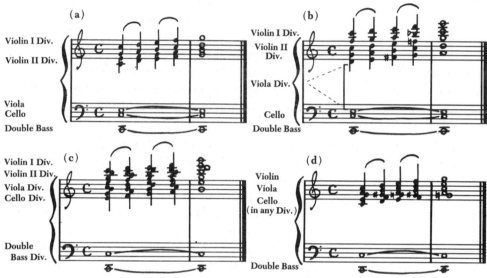

EXAMPLE 46

In each of the arrangements in Examples 45 and 46, the melody is reinforced by other pitches. In Example 46a, the added pitches are the diatonic thirds and fifths above the lower octave of the doubled melody, forming triads. Example 46b makes use of chords in fourths; 46c features dissonant seventh chords. Example 46d shows an arrangement widely used in popular music, and which is not limited to string scoring: each melody tone is doubled in the octave below, and the three other tones of the prevailing chord are fitted in between. Passing tones are usually harmonized with diminished seventh chords.

In each of these four cases the relationship between the melody and the bass establishes the tonality, and these two voices are the only real parts present. The added tones simply add color and breadth. Their identification with the upper melody is maintained by the simple expedient of avoiding any hint of contrast of tone color, and the subdivided strings meet this requirement with ease. This device is one for the composer or arranger, and it is *not* to be considered an available orchestral resource in the translation of piano music into the orchestral medium. It is mentioned here because it should be recognized when it is encountered in scores (if it is not understood as melodic doubling, it may wreak havoc with the harmonic analysis), and because reflections of it appear in music which will be studied later.

Other patterns of string writing are, generally speaking, variations of those already described. Instead of first and second violins in octaves, the combination may be first violin and viola, or first violin and cello. The choice is made on the basis of register and desired richness.

Violas sometimes are used below a cello melody; or they may even supply the bass line in a three-part structure, with first and second violins above.

All the strings may be used on a single line, usually duplicated over three or four octaves; or all but the double basses may be used while these low-pitched instruments join with other instruments in an accompaniment.

Second violin, viola, or cello may be given a principal melodic line even when all instruments maintain their normal relative registers. This technic is more a factor of composition than orchestration, for if an inner voice is to predominate, the other parts must somehow be made secondary. The kind of part-writing which makes this condition obvious to the players results in a better performance.

The strings are indispensable as accompanists to other orchestral sections or soloists. Singly or in groups they provide backgrounds of infinite variety. All the arrangements described above are available as accompaniment, for the string orchestra can be subordinated almost to the point of inaudibility. The careful study of string parts during passages in which other instruments predominate will suggest their versatility.

In addition to their command of the widest range of dynamics, the strings' more specialized resources of tone color have been utilized with increasing frequency during the last hundred years or so. *Pizzicato* — plucking the strings instead of using the bow to set them in vibration—is the oldest and most often used of these devices. It offers a pleasant change of color and is most frequently employed in the bass, to relieve the heaviness that is more likely to be felt there than elsewhere. Its use in the upper instruments is by no means rare, however, and Mozart, in his Flute Quartet, K.285, and Tchaikovsky, in his Fourth Symphony, to name only two instances, wrote complete movements for *pizzicato* strings. Extremely high tones are ineffective when played *pizzicato* because of the shortness of the string. The right hand is normally used to pluck

69

the string, but the left hand of the violinist (rarely any other instrumentalist) can, in exceptional circumstances also be used. The *pizzicato* tone in viola and cello has a slightly longer duration than that of the violin, and this has prompted some writers to require two consecutive tones to a single pluck. They must be quick and fingered on the same string; and even then it is doubtful whether the second tone will project well enough to be heard by the occupant of the last row in the balcony.

Another common resource is the employment of mutes. Their effectiveness decreases as the size of the instrument to which they are applied increases. They make a rather dramatic change in the tone color of the upper strings and are primarily used as agents of color rather than reducers of volume.

Alterations in bowing technic are also used for coloristic purposes. String instruments are normally bowed directly over the *f* shaped apertures cut in the upper surface of the instrument. The effect is roughly that of a farm boy hollering down a rain barrel. The farm boy's voice reverbrates less when he turns away from the rain barrel, and so it is with the violin bow; the tone quality is considerably modified when the strings are bowed away from the tone holes. This device is so special that no universal terms to describe it have evolved. Bowing over the fingerboard is termed in Italian *sul tasto,* or more formally *sulla tastiera;* in French, it is *sur la touche;* and in German *am Griffbrett.* Bowing in the opposite nontone hole area, near the bridge, is indicated in Italian *sul ponticello;* in French *au chevalet;* and in German *am Steg.* When either of these methods of tone production is to be discontinued, either *ord.* or *nat.,* the abbreviations for "ordinary" and "natural" (bowing), appears, and either one, happily, is understandable to most players. No doubt simple statements such as "over the fingerboard" and "at the bridge" would be sufficient to render the orchestrator's wishes clear to English-reading players, but unfortunately this is not yet common practice.

Col legno is the term used to indicate that the bow is turned over and the strings struck with the wood.

The general effect of these bowing technics is one of reduction of brilliance and authority and the addition of an aura of detachment. Their actual effect is indescribable in words (if any musical effect could be absolutely defined in words, the need for music would be eliminated), and only aural experience can demonstrate their individually characteristic sorcery.

After this consideration of their independent or subordinate roles in the ensemble, the individual characteristics of the instruments remain to be discussed.

The Violin. The most brilliant, versatile, and agile member of the group is sometimes called upon to assume the role of soloist. Strings in groups produce a quality of tone unlike the tone of a single instrument. The concertmaster plays alone when the word *solo* appears over the Violin I part, and his individual tone speaks out with as much authority as a solo woodwind, even when the solo violin is accompanied by the rest of the string section. The difference between the tone of the soloist and that of the section of violins is not so much one of volume as of breadth, color, and evidence of personality. The principal player of each string section may be cast as soloist now and then, and the same generalizations apply.

The Viola. The modern viola is a compromise. During its formative years it was undecided as to whether it should be made large enough to efficiently accommodate the pitch depth of its low register or made small enough to be handled like the violin. In the first case, if it were to be built to the proper size, it would have had to be set on the floor and played like the cello. In the end the smaller viola won out; but there is a greater variety of size and shape of the instruments of the viola section than in any other orchestral group. The builders of violas have reached many different conclusions as to how to resolve the conflict between the need for a size large enough for adequate tone quality and small enough for ease of handling. Strange as it may seem, the inadequate size of the viola is an advantage in the ensemble and becomes noticeable only when the instrument is brought very conspicuously forward. The register in which the viola normally operates is rich in audible harmonics, and a rich-toned instrument would constantly call attention to itself, to the detriment of the orchestral balance.

The tone of the cello is as rich as the viola's would be if it were large enough; and it is regularly assigned to this register when it is featured. It is not difficult to imagine what the effect on the ensemble would be if a viola's routine inner parts were sounded with a similar opulence of tone.

Violas are divided more often than the other strings because of their ability to provide a diversity of pitches in close position without the resulting obvious thickness which occurs when other instruments are treated in the same way. A comparison of the effects of thirds on middle C and C in the octave below played on the piano is a reasonable indication of the difference. Violas sound with the clarity of the upper octave when actually playing the octave below.

The Cello. The noble tone of the violoncello has endeared it to the hearts of romanticists, but they invariably fail to say that the cello sound to which they thrill is limited to the upper half of the instrument's range. When the lower register is heard, it is usually referred to as "bass"; this is accurate, but it misleads the innocent music-lover into the belief that the cello is a melodic instrument and the bass is provided by the great big bass-looking double bass. Even a superficial scanning of orchestral scores will show that the cello section spends more than three-quarters of its life providing the bass. The compelling and direct appeal of its melodic appearances may tend to blur an awareness of its normal orchestral function, but the orchestrator must be guided by the requirements of well-balanced orchestral texture. Effective solo colors are everywhere, but the most telling combinations of instruments must be sought out. There is no really adequate substitute for the full-bodied bass of the cello, and it should be—as it has been—used as a melodic instrument only in special circumstances.

The Double Bass. Though usually identified with the cello, the double bass is not a larger-sized version of that instrument. It bears a closer relationship to their common ancestors, the viol family; this is why it is sometimes called the "bass viol." Violin, viola, and cello have quite clearly been established in a separate group, known as the violin family, but the double bass has not to any large degree shared in the modifications of design that makes this identification possible.

This largest member of the string group suffers from a serious disadvantage. It is not nearly as large as it should be for its depth of range; and were it not for its solitariness in the lowest octave, its tone would be regularly overshadowed by those of its colleagues. As is true also of the viola, this lack of an assertive tone is important to the ensemble, because the double bass's normal function is to reinforce the cello in the octave below. Cello without double bass is an acceptable bass; but double bass without cello is almost unheard even in lightly-scored passages. Together they provide exactly the bass weight the world seems to have decided upon as correct for the full orchestra.

Double bass players are expected to match the agility of the cellists in many rapid passages which, if given to double basses alone, would be conspicuously lacking in precision. The thick heavy strings and the wide spaces between steps on the fingerboard might seem to limit the possibility of fleetness; but the skill with which the players overcome the natural lethargy of this instrument is remarkable. It is, nevertheless, most fortunate that their usual location below the normal range of the human voice, makes it possible for us to overlook the frequent departures from ideal exactness of intonation and clarity of articulation.

It should not be assumed that the double bass doubles every note of every cello part, however, for the combination of the two is only the norm of orchestral bass. Double basses may sound only the accented beats or essential harmonic bass tones while the cello plays an ornamented bass line. These double bass tones may be pizzicato or bowed, sustained or short. Now and then the upper bass octave is not found in the cello, but in the tuba, trombone, horn, or bassoon, or even the bass clarinet or harp part. Double basses serve them all with equal effectiveness.

The student who attempts to catalog the repertoire of effective string scoring arrangements and devices will find he has embarked on a life's work, which when presumably complete, will already be obsolescent. The variety of expressiveness of which the strings are capable has not yet been exhausted, and only the complete disappearance of creative originality among orchestrators will prevent the discovery of new musical situations and concepts that depend upon the strings for their realization in sound.

THE WOODWINDS

This diversely colorful assemblage of individual personalities, the woodwind family, brings to the orchestral ensemble resources that are almost an embarrassment of riches. Each member of the group is a soloist who can endow the most mundane series of notes with significance, vitality, and vivid personality. The homogeneity of the string family is wholly lacking, as is also the power of the brass; but the woodwinds are perhaps the most often remembered participants in memorable orchestral moments.

Except for consideration of the range limitations and the efficaciousness of variety, the orchestrator need feel no hesitation in assigning important melodic passages to any woodwind he chooses. They all thrive when in the limelight; it is only in the ensemble that they require special attention. Before we deal with them as an orchestral unit, it will be well to review their most obvious individual characteristics.

Flute. The majority of familiar scores make use of only approximately two of the flute's three-octave range. The lowest part of the range is so easily covered by other instruments that it is useful only in very lightly-scored passages. The extreme high register is shrill and practically unavailable in anything softer than *forte*. Theobald Boehm, whose inventiveness made the modern flute a reality, felt that the high G was the upper limit. G♯, A, and B are now not uncommon, but higher pitches are not very satisfactory. The absolute upper limit is D, but B, C, C♯, and D are uncertain of intonation, harsh of tone, unalterably loud, and uncomfortable and ungrateful for the player. These high tones are used only when doubled in other instruments—only violins and piccolo can extend themselves to this height—in strong passages.

The normal register for flute is one octave above that of the normal range of the soprano voice. When the flute plays in this register, the listener is hardly conscious of the difference, for the flute exhibits none of the tension or intensity of most wind instruments when assigned to the octave above the treble clef.

No wind instrument is more effortlessly agile than the flute; and since there is no reed in his way, the flutist has a ready repertoire of articulations—including the triple and double tonguing more commonly associated with brass technic. The dynamic range is not large, and every orchestral flutist learns to take dynamic markings with a grain of salt. A low register passage marked *piano* may well require almost the maximum of available volume.

Breath control is of greater concern to the flutist than to other woodwind players. The tone is produced by the breath alone, and no reed or mouthpiece-cup is present to direct or channel it. More breath is required to produce a flute tone than seems reasonable, considering the delicacy and lightness of its sound.

Oboe. No orchestral player has as much control over the quality of sound to be produced by his instrument as the oboe player. The tone is very much a result of the player's conception of what an oboe tone should be, largely because oboists spend a good deal of their time making reeds. These reeds are tailored by each player to *his* embouchure, *his* instrument, and *his* particular views on the propriety of the presence of reediness, darkness, lightness, thinness, or heaviness in the oboe tone. A player may even prepare special reeds for the high register, others for the low register, still others to be used on damp days or dry days, and different ones for high and low altitude areas. This preoccupation is probably a reaction to the difficult early years of the instrument's development, when its pitch (and possibly its tone) was apparently beyond control. Evidence of this melancholy state of oboe affairs is still with us, for traditionally the oboe sounds the A to which the rest of the orchestra adjusts its pitch, a reminder of the days when his A was the only one in the orchestra that could not be adjusted to anyone else's.

The double reeds so expertly manufactured by the players vibrate and produce tone practically unaided. The oboist breathes for survival, not to provide fuel for the maintenance of sound. His breathing problem is the opposite of the flutist's.

Oboes were regularly employed in the orchestra when flutes were occasional members and clarinets were unheard of. It is probably this early association that unfortunately has identified them with the exotic East and with the pastoral. The oboe is capable of far more than only this, and serious orchestrators have long made use of its versatility. The instrument is agile enough for the expression of almost any rational musical thought, and its bright, incisive tone enriches strings, complements other woodwinds, and provides a connection between the hard brilliance of brass and the gentle sensibility of the woodwinds.

Its absolute range exceeds its range of characteristic oboe flavor. In the low (lowest third or fourth) register it is likely to become rather overbearing; in the highest register (again upper third or fourth) its tone becomes thin, and loses the piquancy of the true oboe sound.

Clarinet. This late arrival to the orchestra (around 1750 or so) has become one of the most valuable members of the ensemble. Everyone can recall the sound of its not infrequent solos, but its best work is done unnoticed and in support of others. If performances of orchestral works are listened to while only the clarinet parts are followed in the score, their quietly busy career will be understood.

Theobald Boehm's innovations have proved more beneficial to the clarinet than to any other woodwind, for it is now capable of keeping up with the flutes in most situations. Its agility is no longer dependent upon the choice of instrument, and the Bb and A clarinet option may very soon disappear. We are all more or less conditioned to feel a sense of discomfort when the key signature for clarinet contains more than three or four accidentals, but the modern Bb clarinet can successfully manage almost any combination of tones. A glance at the etudes and methods used to train clarinetists will show that the keys of F♯ and Gb-major are not foreign to the instrument.

Alone among its compatriots, the clarinet can produce even its lowest tones with ease and at any degree of volume from *pianissimo* to *fortissimo*. No other woodwind has as wide a range of dynamic level. The high register, above high C or thereabouts, is rather colorless and screechy, but it is still a valuable resource, for without it, the high woodwind colors would be limited to those of flute and piccolo.

Throughout its range the clarinet is available to support strings, other woodwinds, or even brass, or to sing out solo melodies of the most serious or most frivolous intent.

Bassoon. Although the bassoon is kin to the oboe in its use of double reed and its seniority of orchestral membership, its orchestral functions are more closely associated with those of the clarinet. Its tone quality, like that of the clarinet, is perfectly suited to unobtrusive support of the strings; and probably no other instrument takes part in so many passages where the listener is unaware of its presence. It also has a great affinity for horns, and was commonly used as a horn substitute during the period of extremely limited horn technic.

The bassoonist has more serious fingering problems than the other woodwinds, but manages to maintain a fluency of execution equal to the normal demands on the woodwind ·section. The highest register is very awkward for the player and, unlike that of the other woodwinds, lacks intensity. The rich baritone and bass tone found in the lower two-and-one-half octaves becomes rather stark and bleak when the bassoon is forced into its extreme upper range. These top tones are highly effective for suitable, always special, circumstances, but they should not be considered available for routine ensemble passages.

Bassoons stand ready at all times to strengthen a string part or the bass line; to double, thereby removing the brassy edge, strongly scored brass passages; and to serve as the regular low-pitched member of the woodwind ensemble. In addition to these subsidiary roles, the bassoon offers a solo voice capable of a highly diversified range of expression.

Clarinets and bassoons are more important to the orchestrator than basic background colors are to a painter, or articles and atmosphere-setting adjectives are to a poet.

SECONDARY WOODWINDS

The attractive individuality of the tone qualities of the principal woodwinds (or perhaps their lack of homogeneity as a group) has led to the now standard practice of including in the orchestra larger or smaller instruments that duplicate the principal instruments in their methods of tone production and general technic. The intent originally was no doubt to render the special tone colors of the woodwinds available over wider ranges of pitch, but each of these supplementary members established itself as an individual orchestral resource, and each has now been found to have a character and personality of its own.

Piccolo. This small-sized flute can climb to the highest C on the piano. It is similar to the flute in all respects except size, range, and tone quality. Its range, always written one octave below actual sound is one octave higher than that of its progenitor except that, because of the blankness of its tone quality in the lowest octave, it has not been thought necessary to equip the instrument with a miniature foot-joint to duplicate the one used on the flute, and the piccolo consequently cannot produce low C♯ or C. The tone quality is more piercing and shrill than that of the flute and cannot be as subtly used. No matter how much effort is expended by the player, the instrument almost always seems to be playing *forte* in its upper two octaves. The lowest octave is even more impersonal; although it is capable of a modicum of nuance, it is rarely featured. No doubt it is this lack of responsiveness which makes the prospect of playing piccolo so hateful to flutists.

Alto Flute. Far less frequently used than the piccolo, the alto flute (sometimes mistakenly called bass flute) possesses a rich, warm, and communicative spirit. Its rare appearance is probably due to the fact that it extends the range of the flute downward only five semitones, to G below the flute's low C. The high register is poor in tone and in intonation, and sounds like a bad imitation of the principal instrument.

English Horn. This instrument has established itself as a separate entity to a greater degree than the other secondary woodwinds. In construction it is a large oboe, sounding a perfect fifth below the tones produced when the same fingerings are used on the principal instrument. It lacks the low B♭ (sounding E♭ on the English horn). Its characteristic tone is that of the lower half of the range, and higher tones are rather tight and harsh. The highest fifth of its range exaggerates this tightness and harshness, so it is never used where it will be conspicuous. Although it is commonly associated with introspective and nostalgic (not to mention snake-charming) musical situations, discerning orchestrators make use of the English horn's capacity for extraordinary stridency and have used it with excellent effect in conjunction with brass.

E♭ Clarinet. The typical high-register sound of B♭ and A clarinets is implicit in the little E♭ clarinet from its lowest to highest tone. It never approaches the broad, full-throated richness of the principal instrument, even in its lower register.

Structurally, the E♭ clarinet is an exact duplicate of the standard instrument and is as a rule employed only as an upward extender of the clarinet range. It contributes very little in the way of tone color and is valuable chiefly as a reinforcement of the register in which the only other available wind instruments are high flute and piccolo.

Bass Clarinet. The natural bass of the clarinet family is a double-sized replica of the B♭ clarinet, bent at the extremities and provided with a slightly flaring bell, thus making it possible for the uninitiated to mistake it for a wooden saxophone. The increased size applies not only to length, but also to size and weight of keys, length of connecting rods, and heaviness of reed. It is obvious that the bass clarinet is less fleet and graceful in rapid passages than its smaller relatives.

Its orchestral function rarely includes acting as bass to the clarinets. Short solo passages, bass and tenor passages where a bassoon would normally be expected, and general reinforcement service in the ensemble are the everyday occupations of the bass clarinetist. The instrument is designed for richness in the low register, and its high register leaves much to be desired. Indeed, the highest tones are hardly fit for human ears and are never used where there is the slightest possibility of their being heard.

Contra-Bassoon. The relationship between bassoon and contra-bassoon generally parallels that of cello and double bass. Contra-bassoon is the lowest pitched orchestral instrument and is inevitably ponderous and solemn. Eighteenth- and nineteenth-century composers used it fairly often, but seem to have considered it merely a useful way to strengthen the bass line in the *tutti,* which frequently meant doubling the cellos and double basses in rather complicated situations. Nonidiomatic passages abound in this older literature; probably no other instrument has been so consistently misunderstood. Signs of sympathy begin to appear in the latter half of the nineteenth century, and the personality of the contra-bassoon began, very slightly, to assert itself. It is still rare, however, for a contra-bassoonist taking part in a concert that includes three pieces to find three contra-bassoon parts that give evidence of having been written by orchestrators who truly understood the instrument.

The fundamental truths of its capabilities are a tendency to sound lugubrious when called upon to move rapidly, an ability to play only short phrases because of the great supply of breath required to produce the tone, and a good control of dynamic level over the middle part of its compass. The extreme high and low register are awkward, as they are on most woodwinds.

Alone among woodwinds, the contra-bassoon's usefulness as a solo instrument is practically nil. The deep pitches which are its best feature are well below the range preferred for melody.

THE WOODWIND SECTION

It is not possible to classify any of the principal woodwinds as consistently soprano, alto, tenor, or bass instruments. Their roles in the ensemble are wholly dependent upon the limitations of effective range. After the orchestrator has considered these, he assigns dominant or subordinate parts according to his individual preferences, tempered, of course, by his concern for good orchestral balance. Good orchestral balance can be defined only with reference to specific musical situations, no two of which are alike.

The generalizations that follow are descriptions of common practice; they will prove most useful if, when a particular scoring problem is at hand, they are regarded as points of departure rather than ready-made solutions.

A point that should be stressed here is the effect that the development of instrumental manufacturing skill has had on performance. The familiar orchestral literature of the nineteenth century exhibits technics of orchestration that are the bases for all modern practice, but the sounds imagined (and heard) by the orchestrators of that period are not the sounds produced by modern players. Modern flutes—silver, gold, or even platinum instruments—are far more brilliant in tone than the gentle, sweet, wooden flutes used even into the early twentieth century. Nineteenth-century oboists used reeds almost as large as modern bassoon reeds, and their tone quality was broader and darker than that produced by modern players. Clarinets were far less flexible then, both mechanically and tonally, than they are today. Their reeds were made by their players, the way modern oboe reeds are made, and they were fastened to the mouthpiece with string. The control of tone and technic available to our contemporary players would have amazed the clarinetists of 1850. The concept of bassoon playing has been similarly revised; and although the changes wrought are not as drastic as those for the other woodwinds, the modern tone is undoubtedly more positive and incisive than the tone of the past.

Flutists, oboists, and bassoonists now regularly employ the vibrato, and their tones thereby assume a personal, almost vocal, flavor that would have been utterly foreign to the instrumentalists of the nineteenth century. The use of vibrato by an orchestral clarinetist remains an oddity, probably because the instrument's native richness of tone is remarkably cheapened by its use.

American orchestral woodwind players, not obliged to perpetuate a nationalistic tradition of musical practice, have developed versatility of style. European instrumentalists, as a rule, subscribe to national idioms, even when a decision must be made between playing the piece and playing the instrument according to colloquial usage. The French school of woodwind playing is generally recognized as the most highly developed, but no responsible American player considers the French style wholly correct for the performance of American, English, German, Italian, Scandinavian, Russian, Spanish, and South American as well as French music. The woodwind sections of most orchestras are unanimous in their approach to performance, however, and no apprehension need be felt in applying the universally successful combinations described here.

Flutes are bright and clear in their second and third octaves. The lower fourth or so of the second octave is rather easily covered by other instruments, but if care is used flutes will contribute their purity of tone noticeably to the ensemble even here. Oboes are penetrating, especially in the lowest octave. Clarinets are rarely conspicuous in the ensemble; but although their tone is easily obscured by flutes in the upper register and by the oboes in the range common to both, they are strong and valuable in all registers. Bassoons are similar to clarinets in orchestral usage. When secondary woodwinds are used, these relationships do not change. In a routine chord scored for woodwinds, flutes, if they are in an audible range, and oboes will dominate; clarinets and bassoons will provide richness and body. The woodwinds are very rarely used as an isolated section. Solos are frequent, and melodic passages and supporting parts involving two or three members of the group are more often than not present in most scores.

Single Melodic Lines. Two melodic woodwinds playing in unison generally make a poor effect because the individuality of each is negated. The problem of good intonation is very difficult to solve, and the usual result is inconsistency of tone as well as pitch. When an orchestrator uses two of the same instrument, he usually intends to strengthen the line; but, particularly with flutes and oboes, and with upper-register clarinets, the effect is merely one of edginess without an appreciable increase in volume. It is an acoustical fact that two instruments are not twice as loud as one, and miscalculations of orchestral balance cannot be corrected by such doubling.

Melodic unisons of flute and oboe, flute and clarinet, or oboe and clarinet are also questionable. One of them is certain to be in a more favorable register, and the problem of intonation is multiplied because of their different mechanical arrangements and acoustical properties.

The bassoon, because of its range, is rarely available for unisons with other woodwinds. The tones of low-register clarinet and bassoon combine well, but intonation is again a problem.

The range of piccolo is so high and that of contra-bassoon is so low that opportunities to use them for doubling other woodwinds at the unison are rare. When such opportunities do present themselves, they should, as a rule, be ignored. Alto flute, English horn, and Eb and bass clarinets are subject to the same difficulties as their principals.

Melodic Octave Combinations. One of the happiest and most familiar of woodwind effects is octave doubling. Octave flute and oboe, flute and clarinet, and clarinet and bassoon are probably the combinations most frequently heard; but, when the musical environment is appropriate, almost any octave doubling is possible. Three-octave doubling is just as natural to the group; flute on top, oboe or clarinet or both one octave below, and bassoon two octaves below flute occur in many successful scores, and never fail in their effect. As often as not, in classical and romantic scores, two each of flutes, oboes, clarinets, and bassoons are used, the principals all doubling each other over the three octaves and the second players similarly doubling each other on a secondary line, usually a third or sixth below. If the flutes are high enough, it is possible to spread this woodwind sound over four octaves; but this only enhances the effect and is hardly worth seeking.

Chords. The dynamic level must be considered when woodwind chords are scored. Balance of tone can be maintained in a wide variety of arrangements when the dynamic markings are on the soft side of *mf;* but when more volume is called for, the uneven dynamic ranges of the woodwinds impose limitations. The upper-octave *fortissimo* in clarinet cannot be equaled by flutes except in their highest range, and *fortissimo* oboes in their lower octave will easily cover clarinets below their written B on the third line of the staff.

The tone colors of high octave flutes and oboes usually dominate loud woodwind chords, but at lower levels of volume any member of the group may be made conspicuous.

Interlocking is common practice. The simplest pattern, from highest pitch down, is first flute, first oboe, second flute, second oboe, first clarinet, first bassoon, second clarinet, second bassoon. The positions of oboes and clarinets may be interchanged, and such dovetailing may, because of the lowness of range and the need for a clear bass, be abandoned below the fourth highest pitch. If secondary instruments are used, piccolo will, as usual, double first flute an octave above; Eb clarinet will double the melody note in the upper octave (here assumed to be in first flute); contra-bassoon will double the bass tone. English horn and bass clarinet will either double the bass, or other suitable chord tones, or fill in gaps between bass and upper tones.

An isolated chord employing only these twelve woodwinds is not likely to be found; but in general the roles of the individual instruments are as described when they appear in combination with strings or brass, or when they are used in smaller numbers.

Clarinets and oboes may be interlocked while flutes and bassoons are not; flutes and clarinets may while oboes and bassoons are not; or both first and second clarinets may appear below first oboe and above second oboe. First and second flutes may be in unison while the rest of the woodwind pairs are split or while one, two, or all three of them are in unison also.

In soft chords oboe or clarinet may be given the highest tone with flutes providing (not too low) inner harmonies.

Almost any arrangement is possible if it is consistent with the style of the composition and suited to the specific musical situation.

Supporting Roles. Each of the woodwinds is often called upon to reinforce a string part by doubling it at the unison. The woodwind instruments are often unnoticed when doing so, for the string tone remains predominant. The edginess described above as a result of doubling two woodwinds in unison may be here considered an advantage, for if two woodwinds double a single string part, their presence is evident but does not diminish the string tone.

Clarinets and bassoons frequently take part in essentially brass passages; they enrich the texture and soften the tendency toward stridency that sometimes appears in unaccompanied brass.

Flutes, whose limited dynamic range might presumably make their use with *forte* brass impossible, are highly effective when doubling trumpets in the octave above. The flute must be in its highest octave, where it serves as a brilliant reinforcement of the trumpet tone at the second harmonic. Flute and piccolo, because of their clear uncomplicated tone quality in the high register, are particularly useful in this way. The orchestral *tutti* is enriched by these high tones in much the same way that bass lines are enriched by octave doubling in double basses. Other instruments are also used to reinforce stronger tones at the second or third harmonic. Care must be taken that the reinforcing instrument does not equal the fundamental tone in weight or intensity.

Neither woodwind nor any other orchestral section is often heard alone. The normal orchestral tone includes more than one instrumental family, and most passages in which woodwinds predominate are accompanied by string sounds or the combination of horns and strings.

All the woodwind arrangements described above (and many many more) are regularly used in combination with other instruments as accompanists or as conspicuous participants, displacing or doubling one or more of the woodwinds.

THE BRASS

The versatility of brass instruments has been increased since the advent of valves to a point where they are no longer limited to the orchestral *tutti*. They remain, however, the most powerful orchestral group and are able to easily dominate the rest of the ensemble. Because of their new flexibility there is a temptation to treat them as woodwinds, but it must be remembered that both their technic and method of tone production are highly unlike those of the other wind instruments.

A round full tone at all levels of volume and a precision and clarity of attack are the strong points of the brass. The ability of horns and trumpets to hammer out a rapid series of clearly articulated tones has been a boon to writers of fanfares ever since the need for a fanfare was first felt in the human breast. Trombones are not quite so brisk with their triple and double tonguing, but are still quite capable of an impressive display of this technic.

Uniformity of tone and the impersonal dignity of brass instruments make unison doubling quite effective. The woodwinds' diversity of tone quality is not found in brass, and the effects of doubling come close to being what simple logic leads us to expect: an increase in volume and more definitive tone color.

A drastic reduction of color and breadth of brass tone is available through the use of mutes. Mutes are cone-shaped metal objects that are fitted into the bell, but a horn player is quite likely to leave his mute at home and use his right hand instead. Trombonists are less frequently called upon to use mutes than are horn and trumpet players, and the tuba mute is so unwieldy and unsightly a contraption that very few orchestrators have dared to specify its use. The two higher-pitched instruments are far better adapted to mutes and, especially in modern scores, are called upon to use them fairly often. All the characteristic quality of brass tone is lost and a knife-edged penetrating sound is substituted. Extremely high and low registers must be avoided, for the muted effect is minimized when the instruments are not in their middle ranges. It should also be remembered that although muted horns and trumpets are roughly equal to woodwinds in volume, the physical demands on the players are as great or greater than when they are unmuted.

Brass instruments are highly fatiguing to play, and the players' lips are far more perishable than reeds or strings. They must be given frequent rests. Wide leaps are unnatural to brass because all tones are harmonics and the lips (embouchure) alone must find the pitch. High tones are difficult because of the increased pressure and fine adjustment of embouchure required to sound the higher partials.

The brass section as a group provides an homogeneous quality of tone from top to bottom. Either in *piano* or in *forte* it sounds with a breadth and solidity unmatched by any other group. Its power is a resource that should not be wasted; if it is overused, it may become established in the listeners' mind as the norm of orchestral tone, thereby diminishing the effectiveness of strings and woodwinds.

Horn. Four horns were the standard orchestral horn section before valves were invented, not so much because the weight of a quartet was desired but because of the limited number of pitches available on the old hand horn. The four were thought of as two pairs. Twice as many pitches were available if the two pairs were crooked in different keys; in effect, therefore, first and third horns were first horns and second and fourth horns were second horns. The practice of writing first and third horns higher than second and fourth horns remains, and even today the chord

C-E-G-C is written, from bottom to top; fourth horn on C, second horn on E, third horn on G, and first horn on C. Horn players specialize: they are high horn players (I or III) or low horn players (II or IV).

An assistant first horn is a regular member of the section, and sometimes there is also an assistant third horn. All this, plus the use of the double-horn to make high tones more readily available, should make it clear that there is something special about the instrument. The specialness is this: the horn tone the world demands is available only from a tube whose length is far out of proportion to its diameter and to the size of its mouthpiece, both of which are too small. The awkwardness of execution on such an instrument, which is not overcome by any devices to ease the task of the players, has not discouraged orchestrators, who very early recognized the beauty and versatility of the tone quality obtained with so much difficulty.

Horns are as often identified with woodwinds as with brass. They blend with bassoons and clarinets to perfection and are present in most woodwind passages. The romantic era exploited the instrument's effectiveness as a soloist. Oboe and horn in octaves, horn as a member of the three-octave doubling of woodwind melody, unison of horn and cello, horn and bassoon, horn and clarinet; all, and more, such conspicuous uses are common. When not concerned with melodic matters, horns are frequently playing sustained tones or rhythmic accompaniments in the background. In addition to these roles, horns regularly take part in distinctively brass passages.

As in most instruments, richness of tone is lacking in the extreme registers. The horn tone is relatively thin in the topmost tones, and, oddly enough, loses volume and presence. The lowest octave is very unstable, and clarity of attack and range of dynamic level are diminished. It is customary to double horns in these registers except in conspicuously solo passages.

Trumpet. No instrument is more unlike its eighteenth- and nineteenth-century predecessors than the modern trumpet. The tube is only slightly more than half the length of the trumpet known to Mozart, Beethoven, Brahms, and Wagner, and the breadth of tone is undoubtedly correspondingly less. Whether this is an improvement or not is debatable; but the best of our contemporary trumpeters do strive for the broadest possible tone rather than the relatively thin, sharp sound more natural to the shorter instrument.

Tone quality therefore is now a question of the individual player's taste and skill, and the orchestrator who carefully considers the relative merits and qualities of B♭ and C Trumpets is wasting his time. Trumpet players favor the B♭ instrument or the C instrument and will transpose the written part rather than use an unfamiliar trumpet. The little D Trumpet, sounding a major second above the written pitch, is used only when the part lies consistently high, but it is not very common. The reasons for the orchestrator's choice are not considered by the players. In the hands of artists the difference between the two instruments is not noticeable, as the following anecdote illustrates. A world-famous conductor, who was rehearsing a world-famous orchestra, stopped to speak to the first trumpeter. "Are you playing a B♭ trumpet?" he asked. The trumpeter, who was using his favorite C Trumpet, held the instrument high in the air and said, "See?" The conductor was satisfied, and no lack of authenticity was subsequently noted by professional critics or the public. So it goes with trumpet parts. The orchestrator is at the mercy of the player.[2] This is probably the reason why orchestral trumpet parts in general do not utilize the agile virtuosity of the instrument as often as they reflect the classical use of trumpets in the *tutti* and in rare and tenuous roles of atmospheric coloration. Contemporary writers make use of all available trumpet technics, probably because it is one more way to contrast their work with that of earlier masters.

The trumpet is the dominant melodic voice of the modern orchestral *tutti*. Its natural power has made its name a symbol for positive utterance among poets and extramusical writers in general. Melodies for trumpet are quite rare because of the competition of woodwinds, its identification with the *tutti*, and its inevitable outspokenness. Examination of scores will show that trumpets are featured only in large works in which a majority of the orchestral resources are tapped, in passages expressly composed for the instrument and tailored to its personality, or in the *tutti*. These three functions are common to all instruments, but only the trumpet asserts so much absolute authority in them. It is just because of this strength that the trumpets must be used sparingly. They, like trombones, cannot be concerned with trivialities; for if they are given anything trivial to play, the nobility of their character magnifies the effect and the result is the same kind of distortion as would occur if a first-rate orator were to employ his most artful skills in the reading of a third-rate comic strip.

Trombone. For most brass instruments valves were the gateway to full participation in orchestral proceedings, but trombones were chromatically sophisticated long before valved brasses were dreamed of. It is odd that they were not more widely used in early scores. J. S. Bach frequently used

---

2. Even cornet parts are now usually played on trumpets. The cornet is a duplicate of the trumpet except that the bore and mouthpiece are different. Its tone is less brilliant, and even though this gentler tone may be desired by the composer (as in Tchaikovsky's "Cappriccio Italien" and Stravinsky's "Petrouchka") trumpet players consider that their instruments are better suited to the task, and the cornet is rarely seen on the concert stage.

them as alto and tenor voices in his chorales, where only a completely chromatic instrument would do.

Unobstrusive doubling and filling-in, usually restricted to the *tutti* and to very infrequent solo or otherwise conspicuous passages were the lot of orchestral trombonists during the classical and early romantic eras. Many symphonies include trombones in only one or two of their four movements; and even in the movements in which they do play, their role is likely to be small. More recent orchestrators have made greater use of trombones, but even now most of their orchestral parts bear little resemblance to the intricate etudes found in trombone method books.

To the trombonist the ability to produce an absolutely stable, perfectly tuned, full-toned sound in any part of the range without preparation and after long periods of silence is even more important (and more difficult) than technical fluency and fleetness.

The attributes of the instrument are unlike any other. The slide renders it possible for the player to adjust the pitch to perfection, but it also removes any possibility of a true legato. Tones produced when the slide is in its first position cannot be connected to tones of the third position because the slide must pass through the intervening second position. Fundamental skills of trombone playing are the ability to stop the tone (by interrupting the flow of air with the tongue) while the slide is in motion, the ability to move the slide swiftly and accurately, and the ability to synchronize the two operations. Proficient players minimize these short silences to such a degree that a legato effect is almost attained. Even when the slide is moved to an adjacent position (first to second, second to third) the legato is not perfect and the tone is momentarily stopped. The imperfection of legato is disturbing only when it is closely associated with the true legato of other instruments, as in octave or unison melodic lines in trombones and trumpets or trombones and horns.

The trombone *glissando* is rarely used. It is possible only when the slide motion is one-directional. The player can begin the *glissando* on a tone of the seventh position, and, without stopping the tone, pull the slide in through the sixth, fifth, fourth, third, and second, to the first position where the *glissando* must end. The descending *glissando*, even less common, is simply a reversal of the ascending one. The *glissando* may not be continued through all seven positions but may extend from a position higher than the seventh to a position lower than the first. Finally, and obviously, the *glissando* will consist of the same harmonic of each position —if it begins with the second harmonic of the seventh position, it will end with the second harmonic of the first position.

Orchestrators of all eras have called upon trombones when sheer volume was needed. No other instrument is capable of such high decibel delivery, and trombones can dominate the fullest orchestral *fortissimo*. They are also capable of a beautifully controlled *pianissimo*. Solemn and majestic by nature, trombones are even less suited to triviality than trumpets.

It is rather disheartening to examine trombone parts of old scores. So much neglect, so many ill-considered, seemingly last-minute compromises, and such a lack of consideration for the practical problems of the player are evident that one is led to think that trombonists of the past must have been social outcasts, supermen, or nonentities. Anyone who questions the validity of the last sentence need only obtain a score of Beethoven's Ninth Symphony and listen to a performance of the work while limiting his attention to the trombone parts. Modern writers are expected to show a greater understanding of the instrument, and the scores of the last hundred years or so are more considerate of the dignity, character, and idiom of its personality.

Tuba. When the invention of valves made it possible to extend the range of brass instruments downward, the experimentation that took place progressed along different lines in different places. The word *tuba* was applied to valved brass basses in general, and no specific instrument or range was indicated by the term. The modern player consequently selects the instrument best suited to the performance of individual works. It is not uncommon for the orchestral tuba player to equip himself with two or three instruments, changing from one to another as the parts lie high or low.

In most of his work he is associated with trombones, usually doubling bass trombone in the octave below or at the unison, although four-part arrangements are not rare. The tuba is almost never assigned anything other than a true bass line to play, for the great weight and breadth of its tone would be incongruous anywhere else.

The agility of the instrument is remarkable. The long air column can be managed by skilled players, with surprising facility; and though the tuba's performance can rarely be termed graceful, it seldom falls short of the requirements of its role. One limitation imposed by the long air column is the need for very frequent breathing places. Even a legato four-measure phrase in moderate tempo can be a problem for the player.

All orchestrators should be grateful for the availability of the tuba. The early nineteenth-century writers who felt the need for a stronger wind bass were obliged to choose from a discouraging array of contraptions (serpent, ophicleide, sarrusophone), none of which approached the excellence of the modern instrument. Softly played, the tuba blends well with all orchestral groups and can provide a firm, broad, and undistracting bass tone for many combinations. Its more frequent use as the wholly satisfactory bass to the full power of the brass should not obscure its success in more subtle situations.

HARP

In spite of its long and impressive history the harp has no relatives in the orchestra and is an only occasional participant in orchestral music. Its status as a permanent member is due to the fact that when harp sounds are needed, there is absolutely no susbstitute possible. The tone and technic of the harp are unique. Much of the harp's orchestral activity is unnoticed or unrecognized by most listeners. It does not have a wide range of dynamics, and its loudest tone is easily covered by a moderately full ensemble. Much of the impression of *forte* on the harp is due to the presence of so many simultaneously vibrating strings, as in the *glissando*.

The familiar, inevitable, and overused *glissando* is only its most obvious contribution. Harmonic accompaniments to lightly scored melodies are its more usual work. More often than not these accompaniments are arranged as arpeggios covering two or three octaves in one or two measures. After the mechanics of pedaling (which make the harp essentially a diatonic instrument) have been dealt with, harp parts may be written so as to be almost indistinguishable from piano music. Chords of four tones in each hand are possible, but three or two simultaneous tones per hand are most common.

The sound of the plucked harp string is not as short and dry as that of *pizzicato* violins, but it does not sustain as long as the struck string of the pianoforte. If a short, dry sound is desired, the word *sec* is written in the part, and the harpist stops the vibration of the string immediately after plucking it. Because of this lack of legato and the limited volume of single tones, the harp is very rarely used as a melodic instrument. However, it may with good effect double the melody of another instrument, adding its "ping" attack to each tone of the legato tone.

A more important harp function is the reinforcement of isolated tones and chords. Two strings may be tuned to the same pitch (B♯ and C♮, G♯ and A♭) for added weight in such cases or to facilitate the performance of rapidly repeated tones.

Two harps are used primarily to increase volume, and when the two play together, their parts are usually similar. The presence of a second harp also makes possible the performance of passages that, because of pedaling problems, would be very awkward or impossible for one.

PERCUSSION

Timpani. Pedal-tuned timpani are now standard equipment in the orchestra, and it is possible to include them in any passage where their presence is called for. This is a recent development, for many old scores contain places where timpani belong but are missing because of their inability to adjust their tuning to a changing tonality or where they are present but play only where the tonic or dominant is appropriate. The old standard practice of tuning the two drums to tonic and dominant guaranteed their ability to participate in most important sections of the work, but prevented their use in episodes in other keys. Either the timpani were not included at all, or the drums were used whenever one of the two tones happened to fit into the momentary chord as root, third, fifth or seventh. This limitation caused some rather unattractive timpani parts to be written, so that these old scores are not always good models to imitate.

There are, however, valuable lessons to be learned from them if allowance for the intractability of tuning is made. First, timpani are used very sparingly. The intensely dramatic accents that are their chief stock-in-trade become pompous and bombastic if overused. A wise practice for beginning orchestrators to follow is to complete a score in every detail except for the timpani and other percussion parts. Then, the score should be read in tempo, and the places where timpani are needed for emphasis should be marked. A second reading will test the appropriateness of these decisions and should result in culling out a few questionable passages. The actual timpani and percussion parts may then be planned.

Second, timpani are essentially bass instruments. Although classical and romantic scores abound with timpani notes that are not bass tones, analysis will reveal that whenever the bass tone is available in timpani, it is used and that nonbass tones occur only when the need for timpani is so great that their absence would be more noticeable than their presence.

Three tunable drums now replace the old tonic and dominant pair. It is thus no longer necessary to omit timpani in any passages in which they rightfully belong. There is a danger, however, that their new versatility will permit their presence in too many passages in which they do *not* belong. Timpanists should rank high among those orchestral players whose performance time is devoted more to counting silent measures than to playing.

The advent of tunable drums has not altered the essentially diatonic nature of the instrument. The prime function is still to provide a stable basis to the ensemble. A complete and perfectly controlled dynamic range, a vast and precise vocabulary of rhythmic articulations, and a modest variety of tone colors—muffled drums, drums struck with various types of mallets or with the wooden end of the mallet, and drums struck at the center, the edge, or halfway between—are the attributes with which the timpani have won their place.

Other Percussion. Snare drum, cymbals, bass drum, xylophone, tambourine, bells, gongs, and every sound effect from popguns through bird-whistles to thunder and heavy artillery are the responsibility of the percussionists. The list could be extended to include all instruments played with hammers or mallets; but when the celesta or the piano is included in the score, the services of a specialist are usually required.

All the remarks made about the infrequent use of timpani apply doubly to other percussion instruments. When they are used properly, there is no limit to their effectiveness; but even more than with timpani, their misuse can reduce the whole orchestral effect to the ludicrous.

The premodern policy, rarely departed from, of confining the use of percussion to the *tutti* is now thoroughly obsolete. One or another of the large assortment of instruments, or a combination of them, may be used to color, rather than merely emphasize, a rhythmic figure or even a melodic passage. It is hardly possible to describe the multiplicity of effects available from the modern percussion section, for they are limited only by the imagination and discretion of the orchestrator.

STUDIES

1. Examine selected passages from unfamiliar scores. Determine, by studying the individual parts, which instrument or instruments are predominant in sound. Check decisions with recorded performances.

2. Reduce, as the Bartók excerpt on page 63 was reduced, to two, three or four staves the following passages:
(a) Schubert: Symphony No. 8 in B minor, First Movement (below, page 110) measures 63 to 93; measures 345 to 369. (b) Mendelssohn: *Midsummer Night's Dream Nocturne* (below, page 150) measures 16 (with upbeat) to 34; measures 84 to 109. (c) Tchaikovsky: *Danse russe Trepak,* (below, page 168) measures 49 to 57.

Score
Analysis

9

Introduction

*T*HE FIRST CONSIDERATION used in selecting the scores included here for analysis was familiarity. Every record collection should include these works, for each is a firmly established war-horse. It is essential that the *sound* of these scores be indelibly impressed on the student's consciousness.

The second consideration was brevity, for it seemed wiser to include a variety of short pieces instead of one or two extended works. Scores of the twentieth century are represented by regrettably short excerpts. Generally, the great length of modern works and the inevitable restrictions of the copyright laws make the complete quotation of even single movements impractical.

Diversity of style and texture was also sought. Purely novel, unique effects were not.

Whenever possible, two or more recorded performances of each of these works should be listened to. Conductors, orchestras, and orchestral musicians differ, and it is important that the technic of orchestration be distinguished from the effects of individual interpretation.

Invaluable as recordings are, they cannot approach the living, breathing directness of communication of a symphony orchestra in an auditorium designed for concert performance. No electrical or mechanical reproducer of sound, whether it employs one, two, or more speakers, can do more than approximate true orchestral tone. After all, the sound of the string section in the concert hall comes to our ears from an area extending from stage right to stage left. A woodwind solo comes from a single player. These proportions are not clear in recorded performances, and the landscape—or should one say musicscape?—is not always portrayed in true perspective. It is to the credit of the more or less commonly taken for granted composers (here considered as orchestrators), whose compositions are represented in this book, that their works ring true in actual, in recorded, and in read and remembered performances.

Grieg

THE DEATH OF ASE

Peer Gynt Suite No. 1

EXAMPLE 47

THE FIRST FULL SCORE to be studied is an excellent example of careful and effective writing for the string orchestra. It also provides a graphic example of a slight miscalculation of orchestral balance. Grieg's *Peer Gynt* is familiar to all victims of music appreciation courses, and "The Death of Ase" is generally accepted as an inevitable but perfectly adequate illustration of the dramatic situation that gives it its title. The composition calls for five instrumental parts, and Grieg's miscalculation lies in his vain hope that the first and second violins, the violas, the cellos, and the double basses would, for once, add up to that number. Other of his scores show that he knew better; but here, against muted upper strings, he assigns the bass line to undoubled double basses. The total effect of the piece is well enough suited to its purpose, but it behooves us to view it from the standpoint of orchestral efficiency.

The bowing indications are most instructive, for they clearly reflect the dynamic level throughout. Two bows per measure during the first three measures establish the *piano*. The fourth measure implies a diminuendo, for the bows must move more slowly to sustain the tone for three-and-one-half beats instead of the previous two. A *pianissimo* is attained for the second phrase, beginning in measure 4, by reducing the bows to one per measure. Any emphasis on the first note is avoided by the instruction to begin the phrase with an up-bow. This, in addition to frightening the player into an attitude of attention, removes the danger of the accidental accent that could be produced by the weight of the heel of the bow and the player's hand in a down-bow.

Measures 9 to 16 repeat measures 1 to 8, transposed to the dominant key. The *pianissimo* phrase is now marked *mezzo forte*, two bows per measure is continued, and the dynamic markings are more frequent. This succeeds in preparing us for the *forte* in measure 17. Throughout this whole section (measures 1 to 16) an attentive listener will be disturbed by the lack of clarity of the double basses, which are much obscured by the cellos.

A comparison of measure 1 with measure 17 shows that the latter is nothing more than a duplication of the former with each part doubled in the octave. Notice how the bass line now asserts itself as an equal member of the ensemble. One-third of the cello section is enough to effect this change, even though each of the four upper parts is now doubled also.

At measure 21 a *fortissimo* is reached. Each tone receives a long stroke of the bow, and each receives an accent. Reduction to four undoubled lines, omission of the double basses, use of a relatively high cello register, and reversion to the bowing plan of two per measure all aid in the abrupt change from loud to soft in measure 26.

This passage offers an excellent illustration of the characteristic and valuable function of the viola as described in the preceding section. Here the inner voice of the viola is clearly heard but does not overshadow or even equal the vibrancy of tone of the surrounding instruments.

The four-measure phrase is repeated in a lower key in measures 29 to 32, and the effect of the change of register should be noted.

The scoring is rich from measure 33 to 40 because of the solidity of the doubled bass line; but in measures 40, 41, and 43, where the double basses resolve the dominant F♯ to the tonic B and the cellos do not, the effect of resolution is nearly lost because of the greater sonority of the sustained cello F♯. The last three chords will also sound like second inversions (6/4 chords) with a vague rumble below them unless the cellists reduce their tone almost to inaudibility.

This score is worth detailed study, and its good points far outweigh its deficiencies. The composer has, with utmost exactness, indicated every nuance, and aided in their attainment with his careful dynamic and bowing indications. He has also chosen keys and registers that implement the over-all design of varying intensity and quiescence. It is wise for all who orchestrate to observe and profit by Grieg's example.

Schubert

FIRST MOVEMENT

Symphony No. 8 in B minor

EXAMPLE 48

Allegro moderato

°*This low D is below the normal Double-Bass range. It is surprising to find it here, after the care Schubert has taken elsewhere (measures 5, 21, 31, 121, 131, 332) to adjust the bass line to the low E limit.*

111

115

116

127

134

135

137

138

VERY NEAR THE TOP on the best-seller list of symphonies (usually second only to Beethoven's Fifth) is Schubert's *Unfinished*. It is actually only half a symphony, and it is very likely that the composer never heard a performance of the two movements that have become a cornerstone of his reputation. The work was written in 1822, when the limitations of various members of the orchestral ensemble imposed what must have been very discouraging restrictions upon a composer's creativity. An examination of this score will reveal many compromises that Schubert was obliged to make. There are a few miscalculations of effect in it, also, but even so, the sheer weight and breadth of Schubert's unwavering musicality overrides any minute technical flaw. A detailed examination of the first movement diminishes the grandeur of the work not one whit.

The exposition begins with the famous melody stated by what too many listeners refer to as the "basses." This unfortunately means double basses to most of us and has led to much misconception of the role of these instruments. The line is played by cellos doubled as usual in the octave below by the double basses. Who has ever been disturbed by the fact that the octave doubling is abandoned in measure 5 because of the lack of a low C string on the double bass? When pitches go very low or very high (as at the extremes of the piano keyboard), our ability to distinguish fine gradations of intonation or tone quality diminishes. Perhaps the absence of the low D and C♯ in measure 5 does not bother us as much as their presence would. Try the passage on the piano and be honest with yourself.

"When there is no natural line for the violas and you can't bear to leave them idle, double the bass line," may well have been a rule for the orchestrators of the past. In the passage beginning in measure 9, this practice is shown beneath the lightly-bowed, preluding violins.

Clarinet and oboe (measure 13) in unison announce the principal theme. This has often been quoted as an example of Schubert's affinity for and skill with the woodwinds, but I suspect that the loveliness of the melody has beclouded the judgment of the critics. It is, as a rule, unwise to double two single woodwinds at the unison. In this instance it is necessary to listen to a number of performances of this passage. In one the oboe may dominate, for its tone quality is more penetrating than that of the clarinet. In the next the conductor may realize this, and restrain the oboe so the clarinet emerges on top. In the third an equal balance may be achieved. This diversity of effect may be a good thing for conductors who appreciate the opportunity to demonstrate their preference, but it is not good orchestration. The effect is unpredictable, and a fundamental rule for the orchestrator is violated.

Compare measure 20 with measure 230. In the first, the horns and bassoons make a worried little comment, and the lower strings use their bows to sound one urgent bass tone. In the recapitulation the *pizzicato* bass rhythm is not interrupted, the violins are more agitated than before, and the worried comment in horns and bassoons is doubled in the octave above by flutes and oboes.

In measure 26 woodwinds and horns are added to help build up to the climax in measure 29. The second oboe, clarinets, and bassoons reinforce the melodic part (first two of each group of four sixteenths) of the violin figure while the second flute, first oboe, and horns sustain the tone played by violins on the second half of the beats, the stable roots and fifths of the chords. Compare this passage with measures 241 to 244, where the musical situation is the same but the key is changed. The instrumentation is changed accordingly, but the effect remains the same. The horns are omitted, and the sustained tones are given instead to the first flute, the first clarinet, and the second bassoon, and they are spread over three octaves instead of two as before. This phrase is then repeated. This time the horns are included; but because of the dangerous thirteenth harmonic (written high A) they do not double the sustaining woodwinds, but are deflected to the descending melodic fragment and abandoned in the middle of the phrase.

It is also fruitful to examine the two *sforzando* chords for full orchestra as they appear in the exposition (measures 28 and 29) and the recapitulation (measures 243 and 244). The distribution of chord tones is not the same, nor are the double-stops in the first and second violins. The difference in key is responsible for many of the differences, for the limitations of range and in vocabulary of pitches in horns and trumpets make many adjustments necessary. What is the effect of these changes, here and elsewhere, upon the listener?[1]

The horns and bassoons in measures 253 to 257 repeat their introduction to the second theme in measures 38 to 42, but interchange their roles. Schubert was undoubtedly (and wisely) dubious about the horn player's ability to approach the twelfth harmonic (written high G) by leap, and *pianissimo,* in measure 41, although the horn sound is certainly expected at that point.

The second theme is first scored for the cellos in their rich middle register. In the exposition the accompaniment is provided by divided

---

1. The wisdom of revising a score such as this in order to "correct" it for modern performance has often been questioned. It is a decision to be made by the conductor, and careful listening to a number of performances of a single composition will show how rarely an established work is altered in any way.

violas, with the clarinets doubled in the octave above; and in the recapitulation, where the cellos are in their brilliant register, the clarinets, with the flutes doubled in the octave, provide the accompaniment. The bass in both places is left to the double basses, *pizzicato*. The *pizzicato* helps, but the bass is nonetheless weak and inadequate.

The theme is repeated in the first and second violins in octaves. The violas are discontinued (measure 53) because they would tend to obscure the lower register of the second violin, and bassoons are used as replacements. Horns are added, and the cellos are assigned a subordinate role. This makes more obvious the deficiency of the double basses, completely defeated in their attempt to provide a satisfactory bass to the thickened ensemble.

A stark reference to the principal theme (the first two tones) follows the measure of silence. It is scored for the full orchestra, omitting, in the exposition (measures 63-64) trumpets and timpani, but including them in the recapitulation (measures 282-283), where they are able to take part. It may safely be said that no one, not even the player, has ever heard of low C of the flute in measure 64. The flutes play here only as a gesture of unanimity, a common practice in *tutti* passages.

The clarinets and oboes are also in danger of being buried under the weight of horns, trombones, and strings; some conductors, in order to insure that the descending fifths are heard, have the oboes hold on to their C an instant longer than the rest of the orchestra.

Notice the balance and gradations of tone color and weight in measures 73 to 85 and 292 to 304. The woodwinds in two parts, doubled in two or three octaves, the answering of the cello and viola unison by first and second violins in octaves, and the addition of the double bass in the course of the passage are all standard devices and worthy of study.

A *tutti* passage in four-part harmony follows. The harmony is complete in strings and in woodwinds. The brass also have the complete harmony in spite of the awkwardness of the trumpet and horn parts, owing to their limited repertoire of pitches. The timpani is added whenever the chord happens to contain B or F♯. The timpani part is far more satisfactory in measures 304 to 312 than in measures 85 to 93, where the key permits little use of these two tones.

There is also some compromising in the flute part. The first flute doubles the first violin in the octave above most effectively in measures 85 to 93, but has range trouble in measures 304 to 312. Schubert wrote for a flute whose top note was A; and when, in measure 306, the melody ascends to B, the flute is left behind on A, the dissonant seventh of the chord. Many flutists have suspected the A to be a misprint in the part. In measure 310, where the flute cannot ascend to B♯, Schubert does not

144

give him G♯, a tone more fitting than the previous A, but writes the part in unison with the first violins, below the second flute. The passage is completed that way except for one high F♯.

The exposition closes with a contrapuntal treatment of the second-theme motive. The double basses are again left with no one to double, but we do not mind the weak bass so much here as elsewhere. The texture is transparent during the four measures of unsupported bass, and the complex of moving melodic voices is effective. Measures 99 to 104 are a repetition of the preceding passage one octave higher, and it is interesting to see how literally Schubert repeated the lines in different instruments. The first flute replaces the first violins, the first oboe replaces the second violins. The second clarinet and violas replace the second bassoon and cellos. The first and second violins, doubled in part in the first clarinet, replace divided violas doubled in part in the first bassoon. The horns simply rise one octave, and the only unduplicated part is that of the second oboe, which doubles the second violins in measures 97-98. Cellos and double basses provide the usual and solid bass in octaves.

Compare the scoring of this passage with measures 313-323, and listen carefully for the differences in effect.

The cadence in G major (measure 104) is quickly denied by the unison B, and an air of solemnity is re-established by the *pizzicato* strings against the sustained winds.

The development section gets under way with a deflected statement of the opening bass melody in the subdominant. This time the double basses, when their low E is reached, leap up to the cello octave and remain there for eleven measures. The tremolo on the open C string of the cello in unison with the double basses provides a highly charged but dramatically quiet accompaniment to the upper voices.

The first and second violins in octaves (measure 123) softly dwell on the opening motive. They are imitated in canon in the lower octave by the viola and the bassoons. It should be noted that the octave doubling of the violins is here equally balanced by the unison string and woodwind sound below.

Other instruments are added as the *crescendo* grows in force. The climax (measure 147) utilizes all available forces: tremolo bowing in strings, second flute up where it can contribute, interlocked clarinets and oboes, trumpets and horns on their better harmonics, and trombones in their most powerful register. The timpani unfortunately are not included, because neither their B or F♯ fits into the C♯ minor chord.

Measures 151-154 refer to the accompaniment of the G-major theme and the end of the exposition. The serenity and lightness of bassoons in their low-middle register is excellently utilized here. Schubert obviously appreciated the effectivenes of this passage, for it occurs three times (the "legal" limit) without change of instrumentation except in measures 155-157, where the timpanist is able to join in.

Another *tutti* occurs in measures 171-176. It exhibits the standard practice of orchestral *tuttis:* everyone takes part whether heard or not. In this one the tone of the second flute is obliterated by the first violin, the first clarinet and the oboes in unison. The second clarinet, in it weakest register, is buried beneath the weight of middle-range instruments.

First and second violins, and violas in unison, give authority to their agitated line in measure 177, but their dominance is jeopardized by the great weight of the cellos, double basses, and trombones. The woodwinds and horns, with their imitation of the bass in measure 179, are unable to equal the power of the strings and trombones. The superior power of brass over woodwinds is again demonstrated when the passage in dotted rhythm sets in, in measure 185.

The power of the strings is made evident in measures 195-205. Their doubled and redoubled tremolo reduces the woodwinds to an effect of crying in the wilderness, and the assertive and positive second and third beats of measures 203-204 and 207-208 show the strength of the strings spread over four octaves.

The clarinets and bassoons in octave thirds, supported by the horns in octaves, gently seek attention in measures 205-206 and win it in measure 209 as the strings recede.

Flute and oboe bespeak themselves in the approach to the recapitulation. The doubled F♯s, rhythmically unaccented but distinguished from the rest of the passage by their more neutral tone color, lend an air of slight tension to the phrase, which accords with its function of ushering in the return of the principal theme.

Schubert's feat of using the classical orchestra for an essentially romantically inspired work is not the least important reason for the popularity of the *Unfinished.* A modern orchestrator with a wealth of instrumental virtuosity at his disposal would have dealt somewhat differently with a number of situations, but it is difficult to imagine that any "improvement" of this score would increase the power of its personality.

Mendelssohn

NOCTURNE

A Midsummer Night's Dream

EXAMPLE 49

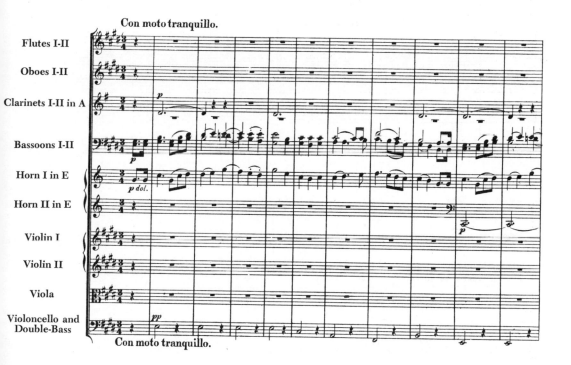

154

IF YOU SHOULD meet a horn player on the street and say to him "Nocturne," he will assume that you are referring to the seventh in a series of nine compositions written by Felix Mendelssohn for a production of Shakespeare's *A Midsummer Night's Dream.*

The principal theme is scored for horn and remains, well over a hundred years after its completion, one of the very difficult and dangerous solos in the horn player's repertoire.

The score calls for a pair of hand horns crooked in E. The first horn is required to produce harmonics numbered 6, 7, 8, 9, 10, 11, 12, and 13. The part for the second horn, the low horn, includes harmonics numbered 2, 3, 4, 5, and 6. These, plus a few other pitches obtained by lowering (with the right hand in the bell) harmonics numbered 4, 6, and 9, make up the horn vocabulary.

The score opens with the solo horn accompanied by the two bassoons. This is a frequently used combination, for the bassoons very satisfactorily approximate the horn sound and in addition provide for more dexterity than may be had from valveless horns. The bass is provided by cellos and double basses in octaves. The clarinet reinforces the bass at the third harmonic, and in general has only sustained tonics and dominants to play throughout the first section of the piece.

The second horn quietly enters in measure 9, doubling the cello for a few measures. He re-enters in measure 16, adding his weight to the *mezzo forte,* providing the bass during the following *diminuendo,* and sounding a low, peaceful dominant pedal point during the latter part of the phrase.

Measures 27 to 33 are repeats of measures 12 to 15 with the addition of the strings. First and second violins in octaves enter unobtrusively with the sustained dominant to tonic. They are simply announcing their presence, preparing our ears for their subsequent leading role, a rather common practice. It softens the effect of the abrupt change to full strings in the following section.

Second violins and divided violas begin an accompaniment in measure 34 before the melody begins. Notice how the melody in the first violin is intensified in measures 36-38. Oboes doubling violins in unison add pungency to the string tone. This is a very effective device, but it is usually avoided in more modern scores, probably because of its close identification with baroque orchestral sounds.

The texture is considerably lightened in measure 39 by means of *pizzicato* cello and double bass and the use of the expressively placid clarinets in thirds. The first horn player views these triplets (doubling the bass tone in the octave above) with a jaundiced eye, for he is a soloist with much challenging work yet to be done. He is very likely to leave this passage to his assistant.

Cellos and double basses resume use of the bow and oboes double the violin melody from the outset of the passage beginning in measure 51. Notice the breadth and richness achieved when the cellos double the violin and oboe melody in the octave below. Also take note of the attention Mendelssohn gives the bass. One or both bassoons are added to the bass line and serve as a reasonable replacement for the departed cello.

The change to lighter texture is again invoked in measure 60; but this time the bright flute tones replace the clarinets, and the clarinets are relegated to the accompanying triplet figure. In measure 62 the flutes and clarinets are unaccompanied, and the clarinets demonstrate their ability to serve as independent, self-sufficient, and unobtrusive accompanists.

In the transition to the first theme Mendelssohn offers, in six measures (66-71), a digest of all the orchestral effects of the preceding section (from measure 51).

The solo horn now returns with the principal theme, accompanied by bassoons, cello, and double bass as before. The accompaniment is highly enriched by the flutes, clarinets, oboes, second horn, violins, and violas. It is no easy matter to accompany a solo with so many instruments; and even though Mendelssohn has carefully placed each accompanying instrument in a well-controlled range, the conductor must be careful at this point. The first and second oboes have the sustained dominant and tonic first sounded by the violins in measures 27-30. Perhaps they are attempting to herald the entrance of the first oboe doubling the horn solo in the upper octave (measures 84-94) as the violins presaged their role in the first part of the work.

All reports about Felix Mendelssohn indicate that he was a gentleman, and his compassion is shown in measures 95 and 96. The horn soloist is given a rest, his solo is interrupted. If he were to continue, he would have been obliged to produce another thirteenth harmonic—dangerous at any time and now more so because of the great effort expended in reaching this point especially after the thirteenth harmonic in measure 89.

The first flute, first oboe, and first bassoon, spread over three octaves, replace the horn, and each is doubled by its second at the third below.

The horn resumes, and it is important to notice how the lead is gracefully taken from him in measures 103-108, where the remainder of the orchestra leads to the cadence. The cadence is obscured by another mention of the principal theme, this time scored more quietly than ever.

The nocturnal flavor of the piece is now enhanced. The flutes in restful sixths and thirds within the octave of the first and second violins, and the motionless first clarinet create a delightful aura of fanciful repose. The first oboe and the second clarinet are subtly added at the dominant chord in measure 117.

In measure 119 begins a passage for first violin and two flutes in a three-part structure featuring the rhythm of the first measure of the principal theme, of which there is a gentle reminiscence in the horn.

The last word is had by *pizzicato* lower strings and the darker toned woodwinds as the first violins sustain their high tonic. Notice the homogeneous quality of clarinets and bassoons doubling the second violins and violas.

The final *tutti* chord is also worthy of study, as is the entrance and departure of each instrument and each combination of instruments used throughout the composition.

Tchaikovsky

DANSE RUSSE TREPAK

Nutcracker Suite

EXAMPLE 50

Tempo di trepak, molto vivace.

Flute I

Flutes II-III

Oboes I-II

English Horn

Clarinet I in A

Clarinet II in A

Bass Clarinet in B♭

Bassoons I-II

Horns I-II in F

Horns III-IV in F

Trumpets I-II in A

Trombones I-II

Trombone III and Tuba

Timpani in G-D

Tambourine

Violin I

Violin II

Violas

Violoncellos

Double Basses

164

165

169

171

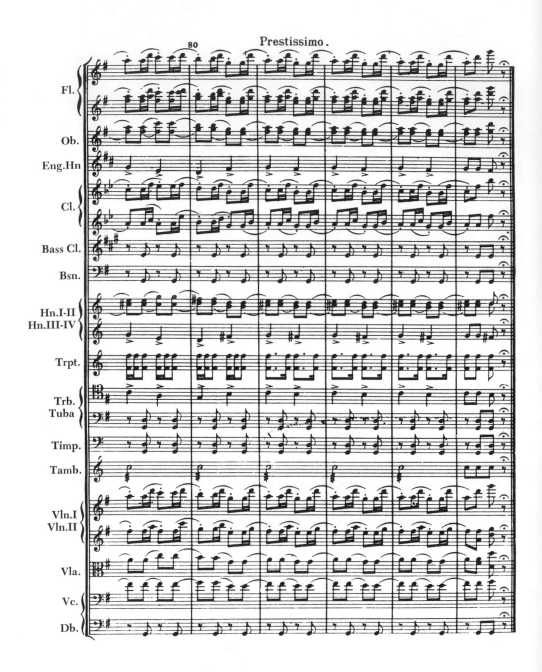

TCHAIKOVSKY'S *Nutcracker Suite* is a dictionary of colorful orchestral effects, quite a few of which should not be imitated because of their unmistakable identification with the original. The complete suite should be studied, for it abounds with examples of beautifully conceived and executed orchestration. Tchaikovsky's rank as a composer may be questioned, but his orchestral technic is unfailingly sure and imaginative.

The fourth piece of the group, "Danse russe Trepak," is chosen for inclusion here because it is an excellent illustration of the use of the orchestral *tutti*. The exuberance of this high-spirited Russian dance, with its forceful rhythm, repetitious rustic melody, and uncomplicated harmonic structure, has prompted the composer to employ the full orchestral ensemble with all stops out. His management of the medium is a model for *tutti* writing in almost any situation, frantic Russian dance or not.

The dance is organized in a simple three-part form. It consists of a principal tune (measures 1 to 8), which occurs six times, and a contrasting secondary theme (measures 33 to 40) which occurs twice and is inserted between the fourth and fifth statements of the opening melody. Eight measures of transition to the fifth statement, and an exhilarating twelve-measure extension of the final statement of the first theme complete the design.

More profitable than a measure-by-measure analysis of the score will be the comparison of the scoring of the recurrent theme that begins the piece. The number of instruments used, and the way they are distributed over the tones of the harmony vary as the intensity of sound increases.

The tones of the first chord are distributed in the arrangements shown in Example 51.

Notice that each of the three versions uses the same pitches except for the addition of the high G in the second and third. The low pitches are separated from each other, as in the harmonic series, and the closer intervals are centered in the middle register. When the high G is added, the upper register is an inversion of the lower: counting up from the lowest or down from the highest, the order of tones is G, G, D. This is an ideal distribution, and it should be approximated wherever a well-balanced and full-bodied tone is desired. However, it is not always possible when the melody, which is usually to be emphasized, is a tone other than the root.

In Example 51a the strings, woodwinds, and horns provide a solid *forte*. There are 15 chord roots present, 7 fifths and 6 thirds. The root is very strongly represented because it is the melody tone as well as the bass tone. The quadruple stops in first and second violins and the triple-stops in viola and cello add to the percussive character of the chord.

175

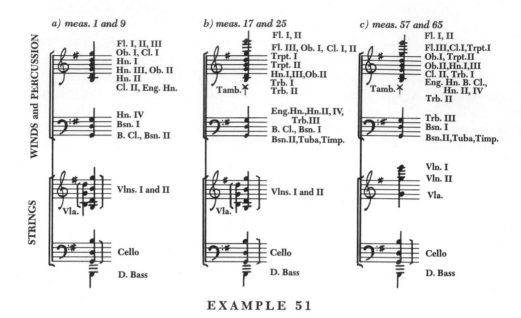

EXAMPLE 51

The intensity is increased in Example 51b chiefly through the addition of the trumpets, trombones, tuba, and timpani. The tambourine adds an enlivening spark. The distribution of chord tones is again heavily weighted toward the root. It is normal to score the complete chord—root, third and fifth in each section in *tutti* passages; but here the third of the chord, B, does not appear in a woodwind. Its presence is strongly felt, however, for the octave between the second trumpet and the second trombone is extremely powerful.

Example 51c shows the chord at maximum strength. Although the instruments employed are the same, and the dynamic marking is unchanged, the sound of this scoring of the now familiar collection of pitches is more forceful than ever. The flutes, bassoons, third trombone, tuba, timpani, cello, and double bass are as they were in the second arrangement. The flutes do not have a wide range of dynamic level and can have no conspicuous effect on a *tutti* as brilliant as this one. Their function here is largely to reinforce the second harmonic of the fundamental in the first trumpet. The bassoons are similarly uninfluential at this high level of volume. The third trombone, tuba, double bass, and timpani are best as bass instruments in all *tutti* situations: changes in their role would lessen rather than increase the effect. The triple-stop in the cello could be discarded without much noticeable loss of effect, and Tchaikovsky probably retained it only to keep the third and fifth of the chord represented in the string department.

The added incisiveness of this arrangement is obtained by the distribution of the remaining instruments. First and second violins and violas, with great authority, sound the melody tone in three octaves. The oboes play the third and fifth of the chord instead of the octave, for oboes in thirds are more spicy than oboes in octaves. The clarinets are in octaves instead of in unison. They have no appreciable effect on the *tutti,* but are arranged this way in order to ready them to double the second violin and viola in the ensuing measure. The English horn is raised from G to D only to give it a higher pitch. When the instruments which double this D are considered, the importance of the English horn at this point becomes debatable. The bass clarinet also becomes slightly superfluous, even though it is raised an octave.

The decisive changes are those made in the brass scoring. The trumpets are high, in their most piercing register. The first trombone is up where a third trumpet would be, and the second trombone doubles the second trumpet as before, but on a higher pitch. The horns too are higher, and it is primarily this greater height of the brass instruments that makes the difference between Examples 51b and 51c.

This survey of three distributions of the same chord is capable of a wide application, for these gradations of the orchestral *tutti* illustrate universal practice. Only further additions of assertive and agile instruments to the orchestra (an unlikely prospect at present) could change the pattern of usage shown here. Tchaikovsky's unerring sense of instrumentation has, in these three chords, utilized the most effective ways to score for the full orchestra wherever either short or sustained full chords, or a drawn-out climactic melody is the subject of orchestral expression.

Just as the scoring of this chord is revised in its recurrences, so are the following phrases.

The melody in measures 1-4 is scored for first violin, and (except for the chord in measure 3, which is another *tutti* punctuation) accompanied by second violins, violas, cellos, oboes, clarinets and horns. In measures 17 and 18 the first-violin melody is doubled in first clarinet and first flute *all'ottava.* The accompaniment is enriched by the addition of double basses, second flute, English horn, and bassoons. The former clarinet part is given to the bassoons, as the clarinets take the former oboe part. The second flute duplicates the second clarinet in the octave above, and the double basses double the second and fourth horns in the octave below. The oboes and English horn reinforce this octave G, first oboe adding the upper octave. Measure 20 is a similarly enriched version of measure 4.

The melody in measure 57 is sounded in three octaves by the first and second violins, and the violas. The first violin is doubled by the first and second flutes, second violin by third flute and first clarinet, and viola by second clarinet. The tambourine may also be considered a melodic reinforcement. High horns and trumpets over the strong trombones add weight to the accompaniment in measure 58.

The parallel triads of measures 5-8 are merely a reinforcement of the melody, not a harmonization of it. They are first quietly scored for low flutes, English horn, clarinets, and bass clarinet. In measures 21 to 24 they are more strongly scored for oboes, English horn, bass clarinet, and first and second horns. Violas and cellos, all four horns, and oboes, in the octave above the strings, are used in measures 61-64. This phrase is used as the extension; and from measure 73 to the end, this triad is arranged with its upper tones as melodic doublings (viola, cello, oboes, and first and second horns) and its lower tone as an almost independent voice (in first and second trombones, third and fourth horns, and English horn). Flutes double the first and second violins at the unison, and clarinets appear in the octave below. Trumpets hammer away at the octave dominant, their rhythmic figure doubled for four measures in the tambourine. In measure 77 the tambourine increases the excitement by abandoning the fixed rhythmic pattern and embarking on a sustained jingling roll.

The rest of the instruments continue their afterbeat tonic pedals. The timpanist is here called upon to strike both his drums at the same time, a rather rare but not unheard of practice.

The contrasting middle section, measures 33-56, remains to be discussed.

The melody is given to the low strings, and the string quality of sound is not disturbed by the doubling in bass clarinet and bassoons. The rhythmic and bouncing violins and flutes maintain the vivacity of the dance. Oboes, English horn, and clarinets provide an imitation of the bass melody and the horns add harmonic support. The third trombone joins in for no apparent reason beyond a desire to keep the pot boiling.

The busy echoing at the end of the bass melody and preparation for the return of the first tune (measures 49-56) is worth detailed examination. Each stringed instrument in measures 49 and 50 is doubled by an unobtrusive wind instrument. Undoubled strings here would be ineffective, because of the contrast between their sound and the rest of the work. The instruments used for doubling do so without asserting themselves or detracting from the string tone, as would flutes in the upper octave or oboes anywhere.

Clarinets, bassoons, and horns are the only instruments to take part in both this string passage and the following woodwind, brass, and timpani chords. In both situations they add to the breadth and solidity of the ensemble, leaving the essential color to be determined by the strings or the brighter-toned woodwinds or brass.

The full orchestra is heard, in measures 55 and 56, in a basically four-voice cadential formula. The distribution of parts, as in the three chords examined at the beginning of this discussion, is an excellent example of what to do when three or four tones are to be effectively distributed among twenty-eight instrumental parts.

This short piece comes close to what is called "bread-and-butter" scoring. There are not many subtleties of effect in it, there are no solo passages, and there is a minimum of independent sectional writing. Each of the devices used here must be a stock in trade of every orchestrator, for they are more frequently useful than almost any other aspect of orchestral technic.

Debussy

Prélude à
l'après-midi d'un faune

EXAMPLE 52

184

186

187

meas. 27

189

meas. 34

193

meas. 48

195

196

meas. 65

199

meas. 68

200

meas. 71

201

meas. 78

203

213

SCORE ANALYSIS

Claude Debussy made his first decisive mark on the musical scene in 1892 with the premiere of his *Prélude à l'après-midi d'un faune.* The work has retained its popularity and is now considered an important landmark in the historical journey toward modern music. The style, the musical expression of impressionist painting and poetry, is its outstanding characteristic. Harmony, form, and orchestration are secondary to, and even obscured by, the stream of semi-consciousness depicted.

Trumpets, trombones and tuba, timpani, and percussion (except for a pair of tiny tuned cymbals, which are used only in the final ten measures) are omitted, for it is their habit to speak with positive and authoritative voices. In this limpid score the most exotic aspects of orchestral sounds are masterfully utilized, and these special and fragile effects would be dangerously minimized if obliged to compete with the full orchestral *tutti.* The composer has used the instruments best suited to the dynamic levels and variety of tone color required for the precise portrayal of the musical idea.

Just as horn players react to the word *nocturne,* so do flutists understand the word *afternoon,* for in this score Debussy has made frequent use of the expressive lower half of the register in some of the most telling and gratifying passages in the flute repertoire.

The opening solo, followed by the harp *glissando,* woodwind chord, and pastoral horn, sets the atmosphere of the whole work. The key signature is E major, but neither the flute melody nor the first chord we hear establishes that or any other key. The expectation of regular form is at once destroyed by the pause (measure 6) and the lingering on what should have been a cadence but isn't. Tonality and form being thus disposed of, the style, brilliantly conceived and maintained throughout, captivates the listener and holds his attention to the end.

The technics of orchestration as applied in this new style are forerunners of many modern practices. Noticeable among them is the deliberate utilization of instrumental characteristics that had hitherto been generally considered weak spots, such as emphasis on the clarinet throat tones and the low register of the flute. Subdivision of the strings, while hardly a new device, is here used not for increased breadth of string tone, but for color. Indeed, every combination of sounds Debussy used is the result of the stylistic need for diversity of color; and the woodwinds (with horns), whose specialty is just that, are absent in only one of the 110 measures of the piece. They are entrusted with every important melodic member of the composition, and, with harps, provide and enhance the essential impressionistic atmosphere.

Performance of this work is not easy for any orchestra, for it never plays itself. The strings must find the proper times and degrees of subordination, for they are usually assigned an accompanying role. The woodwinds must alternately blend perfectly with each other, come to the fore as soloists, and assume an unobtrusive position as accompanists. None of these functions is made obvious to the players, for musical notation has not developed to a point where melodic passages can be designated as dominant, secondary, or reinforcing. The impressionist style points up this deficiency of notation, for although tone quality is the important element, the pitch and contour of the line do not serve as clues to the *degree* of prominence to be given to the written notes.

The conductor's artistry is also called into play by the need to rectify or compensate for certain questionable episodes in the orchestration. These episodes will be revealed by the ensuing technical analysis of the score. In this, as in our other dissections of important works, it must be remembered that one or two slightly askew strokes of the brush do not lessen the total effect of a masterwork.

The written phrasing is no help to the flutist in the opening. There is no breathing place indicated, and the implication is that the whole phrase should be played in one breath, by no means an easy accomplishment. The flute solo beginning in measure 21 continues to the fourth beat of measure 27 with no breathing place clearly indicated. It is interesting to see the way different flutists cope with this problem.

The few pedal indications in the harp parts in the score do not appear in the players' copies. There is no apparent reason for this sporadic appearance in the score.

The string tones are minimized by mutes *(sourdine)*, subdivision *(divisi)*, and by bowing over the fingerboard *(sur la touche)* away from the *f* shaped tone holes. The chords of the second harp in measures 5, 7, and 8, the soft throat tones of the clarinets in measure 11, and the low flute solo (11 to 14) would not be so clearly heard if the strings were unmuted and bowed normally. In measure 17, the principal melodic line is given to both oboes doubled in the octave below by both clarinets. This is a rather sharp, incisive sound, and the strings revert to normal bowing *(position naturale)* in order to hold their own in the rich complex of melodic and accompanying wind instruments. The second and third flutes (marked I and II because they are first and second on that line of the score), English horn, two bassoons, and the two high horns would very likely cover the string tone of the preceding six measures. The mutes are retained, however, and even the entrance of the first violins divided in octaves in measure 18 does not give the strings dominance over the winds.

The next flute solo (measure 21) is very lightly accompanied. Cello and horns (the horns are notated in the old-fashioned way: they sound the E *above* the written B) sustain the finally arrived at root and fifth of E major, punctuated by the *pizzicato* double bass; and the harps provide a gentle surface ripple that perfectly complements the long C♯ of the flute. This recurrent use of the flute's middle C♯ is no accident, for it is probably the most flexible tone on the instrument and gives the individual performer the opportunity to color it as he will.

Debussy finally remembered that flutists require opportunities to breathe, and in measure 27 assigned a portion of the melody to the second flute in order to give the first flute a short recess.

The strings have been stirring since measure 22 and by measure 28 have grown strong enough to require an increase in the counterbalancing woodwinds. Debussy's solution was to use two flutes instead of one on the melody, and it is his first mistake. Doubling woodwinds, especially flutes and clarinets, at the unison does not noticeably increase volume or breadth or weight of tone, but only points up the fact that pitch and nuance in woodwind instruments are solely dependent upon the individual performer. No two performers (or instruments) can possibly be completely in accord on these matters, and the result of such doubling is only to eliminate the evidence of personality and produce an all-too-frequent lapse of good intonation.

Also noticeable here is the imbalance of the strings. Even though the cellos are divided, they still outweigh the double basses. The true bass line of the ensuing passage is not clear, and in many performances goes unnoticed.

Muted horns and a now unmuted cello section accompany the entirely throat-register clarinet in measure 31. The harp, second violins, and violas are only atmosphere—impressionist coloration.

The general tone has until now been a legato and lyric flow of melos; but beginning in the cello, measure 31, crisper sounds are heard. *Pizzicato* strings and brittle harp tones disturb the naïveté of the whole-tone scale figures in clarinet and flute and the clarinet's restless version of the opening motive.

The first oboe, solo, enters assertively in measure 37, and when the violins (measures 40-41) imitate this melody, they are accompanied by both oboes and both clarinets in octaves. The accompaniment, F♯, F♮, E, is only an imitation of the preceding measure in the second violins and cellos. The woodwinds, here, doubled as they are by the cellos in measure 40 and by the first horn in measure 41, are quite capable of overbalancing the violins. Clarinet and flute an octave above add their version of the current melodic figure in measure 42, and the violins echo it in measure 43.

The management of the clarinets at the key change is rather peculiar, and though not without precedent, it is hardly reasonable considering the era of the composition. Clarinets in A have been employed up to this point, but here the composer considers it wise to change to clarinets in Bb. The oddity of this decision will be apparent if we trace the clarinet parts to the end of the composition. The first clarinetist is given a scant two beats in which to change instruments. He is then confronted by the wrong key signature. The signature for Bb clarinets in measure 44 should be two sharps; instead, three flats, the correct signature for A clarinets, are there. In measure 51 the signature changes again, but not for the clarinets, who continue with their three flats as though no change has occurred. In measure 55, the key of Db major is clearly proclaimed, and the correct signature is given to all; the three-flat signature for clarinets is at last justified. In measure 79 the tonality returns to E major; but rather than write six sharps for the Bb clarinets, Debussy cancels all accidentals and gives them no signature at all. When C major prevails (measure 83) and the clarinet signature should again be two sharps, the signature of no accidentals is retained. The players are instructed to resume the use of A clarinets in measure 90; and when the tonality settles down again (measure 94), they are given the correct signature of one sharp. Any competent clarinetist of our day can play this part without undue difficulty on either the Bb or A instrument. Before the advent of the Boehm system of key mechanism, some of the chromatic passages in the throat and across the break would have been very difficult if the designated instrument were not used; but even so, the choice of key signatures is inexplicable. Perhaps the composer foresaw the modern practice of using no key signature for music of constantly shifting tonality, but why would only Bb clarinet players be given the role of prophet? Since the score indicates that the change from A to Bb clarinet is to be made in only two beats (a highly conjectural possibility) it is reasonable to suppose that Debussy did not seriously consider the mechanics of performance, but was making an inept gesture toward conventional usage. The net result of this strange notation is that the parts must either be read with reference to an unconnected group of accidentals (the wrong signature), or, as in the horn parts, with the accidentals of the key signature inserted in the part as occasional chromatics. If the student will adjust himself to this troublesome task, we will return to the examination of the score.

In measure 44, flute and oboe in unison, a rarely satisfactory sound, and clarinet and bassoon in octaves vie for the limelight. In the second half of the measure the second oboe is added in the octave below the first oboe, and second clarinet and second bassoon double their principals at the unison. English horn doubles the bassoons, and the woodwinds become quite heavy. They can easily dominate the strings in measure 45, even though the viola is doubled by the third horn, and the conflict between the woodwinds and the violins obscures the unsupported cello. The scene is gradually cleared as violins and horns (measures 47 and 48) give way in measure 50 to the distant sound of flutes and the first harp doubled at the unison by the harmonics of the second harp.

The throat register of the clarinet is again featured in measure 51, and the four- and three-part chords assigned to the violins must be held to the background. The doubling by the horn does not make this easier, but does maintain the impressionistic flavor of flickering shades of tone color.

Debussy unfortunately gives the show away in measures 53 and 54. His apparent attempt to portray the dappled light and shadow of the Faun's idyllic environment results in an irritating sense of out-of-tuneness in the woodwinds. The first oboe joins the clarinet solo at the unison, and the second flute (no doubt representing the sunlit spots) plays every other tone, also at the unison. This is tone-painting carried to the extreme—the extreme at which the theory exceeds the limits of practicality.

An example of sectional opposition occurs at the key change to D♭ major. The wholly woodwind melody is accompanied by divided strings and unobtrusive bassoons and horns. The woodwinds are not as evenly balanced as are the strings, and it is a moot point whether Debussy sought the effect attained here, or, desiring unity of woodwind sound, he uncritically wrote this melody for them as though they were capable of consistency of sound as are the strings or the brasses. Even casual listening to this passage exposes the unevenness of the woodwinds. Clarinets and oboes are most evident at the beginning of the passage, but at the low F in measure 56 and in all of measures 59 and 60 the self-sufficient and very outspoken English horn and oboes push the other, gentler woodwinds into almost inaudible subordination. The flute makes its presence felt in the higher-pitched regions of the melody, but even the addition of second and third flutes does not equalize the balance. The first horn joins in (measure 61) and contributes a rich and welcome stability to the melody. Although the horn is doubling the woodwinds, the composer has not indicated in its part the one-measure (61) *crescendo* or the word *subito* (suddenly) at the *pianissimo* in measure 63. Such trivial inconsistencies are little riddles for the conductor to puzzle over.

The D♭ melody is now scored for strings: first and second violins replacing first flute, first oboe, first clarinet, and violas and cellos doubling in the octave below where second clarinet and English horn were. The evenness of string tone during the second occurrence of this melody is a marked contrast to the disparate tone qualities of the massed woodwinds.

The accompaniment is enriched by the pulsating winds and doubled harp arpeggios. The impressionistic paintbrush is again applied to point up subtly a mild highlight in measure 64, where the oboes replace the clarinets.

The *crescendo* beginning in measure 65 reaches a climax in measure 70, and the full complement of instruments is employed as follows: the principal melody in measure 67 is given to the strings as in the preceding four measures. The bass is assigned to double basses and second bassoon. The double basses are divided in octaves when the bass tone is G♭ and are in unison when E♭ is bass. When the double basses are in unison on E♭, the fourth horn is called upon to provide its upper octave. Buried as it is under the mass of orchestral sound, it is unlikely that this little subtlety is ever noticed by the listener, but it is another indication of the impressionistic effort to preserve balance while constantly varying the lights and shades of tone color.

The pulsating motive of measure 63 grows more melodic in character in measure 67. It is now scored over three octaves in first flute, both oboes, English horn, second horn, and harps. Second and third flutes, first and second clarinets, and first and third horns provide harmonic support to this secondary melody.

The melody in the strings is easily obscured by the weight of the accompaniment, and Debussy's indication of *fortissimo* for the strings and harps and *forte* for the winds does not guarantee good balance.

In measures 71-74 the *diminuendo* is accomplished by the obvious combination of dynamic markings and the use of fewer instruments.

Horn, clarinet, and oboe, reminiscent of previously heard melodies, accompany the concertmaster's solo violin in one last subdued and intimate version of the D♭-major melody.

A quasi-recapitulation is effected in measure 79. The solo flute plays the opening motive, now in E major and accompanied by sustained chords in muted strings and harp arpeggios. Sharp contrast to this peaceful passage follows, and the staccato of the low register oboe, tremulant clarinets, bassoons and horns, and *pizzicato* strings cast a momentary shadow over the landscape. It is dispelled by the graceful downward flutter of the wind instruments in measure 85. These two sections (measures 79-85) are repeated with modifications. First oboe replaces the solo flute in measures 86-89 and English horn replaces oboe in measure 90. The downward-sweep figure is fragmented, and the flutes are followed by strings instead of the other winds. Harp *glissandi* are inserted, and doubled horn and English horn decorate the picture with a single striking note (measure 92). The horn part is marked *cuivre*, an instruction to the player to produce a metallic quality of tone. *Bouche naturale* in measure 93 instructs him to resume the normal method of tone production.

Very few conductors can resist revising the score in measures 94 and 95. Debussy has written the flute solo passage for both the first and second flutes, thereby losing all the individuality of expression that it calls for, that it has received at each preceding occurrence, and that is an integral and salient characteristic of the work. One flute is frequently used, a far more satisfactory sound. The accompaniment is a featherweight string tremolo, muted and again *sur la touche*. The antique cymbals are introduced at this point, and provide a delicate bell-like tone. They do not sustain their tone for any appreciable length of time; and Debussy wrote dotted whole and half notes for them, understanding, it may be supposed, that their effect is made at the instant they are struck together.

Two unmuted solo violins enter in measure 95. They, in octaves, play a modified form of the motive that has previously been heard in various instrumental arrangements and degrees of importance (measures 39, 40, 47, 51-54, 67, 69, and 74).

In measures 96 and 97 the flute melody is a motive derived from the second phrase of the Db major melody (measures 61-62, 68 and 71-73). It is scored for the rather harsh-sounding combination of two flutes and one oboe in unison. The solo violins are now joined by a solo cello and both clarinets in the octave below the second solo violin. In performance this page is enigmatic, for if the flutes and oboe are brought to the fore, their incompatibility as co-soloists is emphasized; and if the violin solos, clarinets, and solo cello are featured, the continuity of melody is endangered. The listener's attention is usually drawn to the flute and oboe melody, for it is now familiar, but its voice here is not pure enough to convince him that he has not been misled. (Blurred edges are a feature of impressionistic art.) The accompanying body of muted string tremolos *(sur la touche)* and other supporting sounds save the situation, for they maintain an attractive and stable foundation over which the conductor can attempt to establish an effective balance of the two melodic elements without endangering the basic orchestral tone.

The first flute is restored to its rightful status as soloist in measures 100 and 101. Here it is effectively doubled in the octave below by a solo cello, and the accompaniment is a beautifully balanced and colorful background.

The measure marked *Retenu* (102) seems to be a halting and exhausted summation of the work. The fragment of melody in oboe, the repetitious flute, and the hollow intervals between flute and English horn predominate.

Solo oboe interrupts boldly, extending the second half of the opening phrase (measures 3 and 4). This leads to the first real cadence in the tonic key. As flute and oboe approach this cadence in a downward direction, the strings (divided first violins and the solo cello) strengthen the effect of its inevitability by leading to it from below. There has been no such conclusive cadencing before this, and we accept its finality without question. It should be noticed that this is in no way a result of orchestral technic, but is a manifestation of the composer's complete control of design, timing, and balance and contrast of mood.

The harps seem to rebound off the center of tonality, accenting it as they do so. The four measures that follow are mere reflections of the cadence. Reflections are a feature of impressionist art, and they are here portrayed with true impressionistic artistry—almost bizarre coloration, yet somehow a perfectly realized picturization of the scene.

The three-part harmonization of the opening motive, scored for two horns and muted violins, is unprecedented. Harp harmonics, *pizzicato* low strings, muted violins, and the remote and gently punctuating cymbals as accompaniment to the low flutes bring the piece to a close without the vaguest suggestion of any violation of style.

The analysis of this score, and of the others included in this book, should demonstrate that orchestration is only a means of communicating a musical idea. Technical defects, such as minor miscalculations and instrumental limitations, do not seriously disturb this communication. It is the expression of the composer's essential idea which every orchestrator should strive for.

The Twentieth Century

MODERN MUSIC, however enigmatic much of it is to so many sincere lovers of music, is less baffling orchestrally than in some of its other aspects. The instruments employed are still those which were familiar to concert-goers well before the turn of the century, and the fundamental technics remain unchanged.

The many advances in instrument manufacture and the virtuosity of our leading orchestras have made it possible for orchestrators to make greater use of extreme register tones and more subtle combinations of instruments. Most instrumental sounds are now more brilliant than before. The bows and bridges of the strings, the bells and bores of the winds, are designed for maximum power as well as for accuracy of pitch and ease of control. The wind instruments have been more affected by this tendency toward large sound than have the strings, and the string section is now easily dominated by the winds.

The advent of valved brass with their new flexibility and the availability of tunable timpani have led modern orchestrators to make use of those instruments to a degree undreamed of by their predecessors. A new spirit of radical experiment in the search for new sounds has established the tone qualities of low-register piccolo, high-register bassoon, muted brass, and multi-divided strings as commonly accepted and normal orchestral resources.

Orchestration has become a separate field of musical study. Where formerly composers were obliged to learn to express themselves in spite of the orchestra, many contemporary practitioners are able to use their knowledge of orchestration as springboards to creativity. Others, overawed by the apparently unlimited resources of instrumental proficiency, are prone to exceed the bounds of practicality. Even the most skilled performer will complain about some modern writing, for there are works in the current catalog that contain a discouraging number of instrumental impossibilities. To mention but one example: C below middle C, and an

223

altissimo C, five leger lines above the treble clef marked *dolce,* are written for clarinet in a well-known score. Such instances are the exception rather than the rule, however; and no period of musical history has witnessed as much attention devoted to the orchestral medium of expression as our own.

The four scores chosen to represent the modern era, even if quoted in their entirety, could not be expected to illustrate every modern device. The range of expression of the orchestra is limited only by the talent of the orchestrator. Ravel, Stravinsky, Hindemith, and Bartók have produced complex and personal masterpieces of musical utterance, each in his own individual language, yet each using the same general complement of instruments. Ravel's alto flute, Stravinsky's orchestral piano, Hindemith's use of the orchestral recitative, and Bartók's reaching to the remotest corner of the orchestral storeroom of color are typical, but not necessarily definitive, of twentieth-century practice.

Copyright restrictions prevent more extensive quotation than the excerpts reproduced here, and it is hoped that the glimpses into these scores will whet the student's appetite for more thorough study. Even these fragmentary passages, however, exhibit many characteristic contemporary practices, not the least of which is accuracy of notation. Ravel's use of the divided string section as a single melodic unit, Stravinsky's use of many different instrumental tone colors to sound a single melodic line, and Bartók's use of radically contrasting textures and colors in close juxtaposition may be mentioned as particularly noticeable departures from nineteenth-century practice.

Not evident in such brief extracts is the consistency and individuality of style maintained from beginning to end in each of these works. The larger palette of colors and wider dynamic range of the twentieth-century orchestra have not blurred but rather enhanced the individual personalities of these composers.

Ravel

Daphnis and Chloe Suite No. 2

EXAMPLE 53

227

230

RAVEL WAS AS meticulous a workman as ever put pen to score paper. The most detailed, complex, and subtle devices of instrumental usage are conceived, realized and notated with pristine clarity in his work. His command and utilization of orchestral resources is so outstanding in this and other of his works that the abstract musicality of his conceptions is sometimes overlooked.

The passage under consideration here, score pages 41-45, begins with a phrase for two oboes and English horn. This type of three-part passage scored for three instruments of one color in partially responsible for the increase in the use of the secondary woodwinds. Harps, muted violins and violas, and low flute provide the accompaniment, an assortment of F♯s. The almost finicky arrangement of harmonics in strings and harps is typical of Ravel's attention to the most subtle gradations of color. The G♭ instead of F♯ in harps is used because harp strings vibrating at maximum length, their flat position, are more sonorous than when shortened by the pedals to produce the natural or sharp positions. The still muted strings echo the woodwind phrase. Viola harmonics and harps are in the background; and in the last two measures of the page, piccolo, first flute, and harps combine to vary the sound.

Pizzicato strings and muted horns under the light and quick harp *glissando* on the last eighth-note of the measure usher in the oboe solo at measure 174, followed by the solo flute. The across-the-strings *pizzicato* in the first violins and violas and simultaneous *portamento* (string *glissando,* executed by sliding the finger along the string) in the second violins and cellos provide a startling lift before the *fermata.*

The clarinet (in A) solo is similarly introduced, and is followed by English horn, as the oboe was previously followed by flute. The oboes complete the English horn passage with an upward scramble in imitation of the *portamento* in the strings.

C♯ is announced as the accompanying note by cellos, double bass harmonic, and first bassoon. It is duplicated in the upper octaves first by piccolo and first oboe in octaves, followed in the octave below by first flute and English horn in octaves, and continues its descent, *diminuendo,* until it reaches the register of its first appearance in cello, now heard as a harmonic in that instrument, doubled in the lower octave as before by the double bass harmonic.

The harps are conspicuous, for the first harp is the constant factor in the falling and fading C♯. Both harps are used to double piccolo and oboe, and each, having tuned the D strings to D♭ and the C strings to C♯, contributes two notes to each octave. In accordance with the dynamic markings, the second harp is discontinued, and the first harp ceases the doubling of the C and D strings.

Violins and violas here sound with a breadth and richness that has been widely imitated in commercial music circles. The melody, in the upper first violin, and the accompanying C♯ form an inverted dominant seventh chord of D major. D is the tonal center here and in the part preceding our quotation.

Each tone of this melody is doubled at intervals that combine to form a dominant seventh chord of which the melody tone is the root. This parallelism is an important device and may be considered either·a harmonic procedure or a coloristic resource. The chord in other situations may be any triad or seventh chord; if only two instruments take part, it may be any interval. The most important concern should be that the doubling voices do not stand out as independent parts, but are rhythmically, melodically, and coloristically identical with the principal melody, as here. They differ from the melody of the upper first violin (doubled in the octave below in upper viola) only in pitch. The doubling often includes cellos as well in other sections of this score and in other compositions.

Clarinets, bassoons, and muted horns take up the final chord of the string passage and raise it a major second to reveal the C♯ as the dominant of the coming F♯ minor section.

The beautifully effective flute solo featured after the key change is accompanied by an intricate and fragile arrangement of strings, harp, and horns. If all these tones were played on the piano, the result would be harshly dissonant; but Ravel's instinct for orchestral balance and distribution of color blends them into a perfectly weighted accompaniment.

The flute solo is made of tones of the tonic (F♯ minor) chord and scale, accenting the ninth, and including (in the last measure quoted) chromatic passing tones. The accompaniment consists of the German sixth of the key over the double pedal point, the alternating tonic and dominant in the *pizzicato* double basses. The augmented sixth (B♯) of the German sixth is spelled C♮, probably for ease in reading. It resolves to C♯ in the measure following the excerpt reproduced here.

The chord is sustained in second violins and upper violas, as first violins and lower violas play it in guitar-like *pizzicato* on the second eighth-note of each measure.

The dissonant C♯ simultaneously sounded with the C♮ and D of the violins and violas may be explained as a dominant pedal point or as a reinforcement of the double bass F♯ at the second harmonic. Like the chord in violins and violas, it is both sustained and short. *Pizzicato* cellos and doubled harp harmonics join the violins and lower violas on the afterbeat, and one horn sustains.

The horn players, having recently removed the metal mutes (*sourdines*

233

in French) as instructed, are now directed, by the little cross beneath the notes, to mute their instruments by hand. Since they cannot sustain tones for long periods of time, both the second and fourth horns are employed in alternation. They spell each other, and the change is made where it will be least conspicuous: with the *pizzicato* of the strings.

Stravinsky

DANSE INFERNALE
DU ROI KASTCHEI

Firebird Suite (1919 Version)

EXAMPLE 54

237

239

Stravinsky's two ballet suites, the *Firebird* and *Petrouchka,* have won a place in the standard orchestral repertoire because they combine novelty, innovation, and daring with characteristics that have a more permanent appeal to the musical public: originality, vitality, and lasting freshness.

The fragment reproduced here, measures 20 to 36, is a midpoint in the working up of a general melée. The assertive and anticipatory events shown in these few pages are typical of the air of excitement that Stravinsky generates: his scores are often more complex, rarely simpler. Special, off-the-beaten-track devices of instrumental practice are frequently found in his scores, but they are always used to good effect. He seems to have adopted a policy that requires each player to be alert and ready to deal with the bizarre at any moment, yet he rarely departs from what skilled players consider to be idiomatic part-writing, difficult as the parts may be.

A comparison of the horn and violin parts in the first measure of our excerpt illustrates this point. The conclusion of the current motive is seen in the horns. The first and second play it in octaves, as the third and fourth bite off the same pitches and the tuba adds his weight to the last two tones. The string parts are in essence doubling this melody. The second violin doubles third and fourth horns in the upper octave, but first violin and viola each seem to be trying to play the same melody in two octaves at once. The cello is busy maintaining the rhythmic pulse while carefully bowing and fingering alternating natural tones and harmonics, and the double bass is called upon to produce harmonics.

The timpanist, directed at the outset (or onset) of the movement to use wooden sticks instead of padded mallets, contributes to this undercurrent of restlessness.

The *tutti* interval (not a chord, because only two tones are present) conveys a feeling of tension, not only because of the driving nature of the work, but also because so many instruments are summoned to their highest register. Piccolo and flute players, who have no difficulty with high isolated *forte* tones, are given a flourish of grace notes to keep them busy. First oboe and first clarinet (in A) are almost at their highest extremity. First and third horns are dangerously high, and, against the strength of trumpets, trombones, and tuba, can contribute little other than a sense of their danger. The string players are also confronted by a situation that requires more attention than the usual tutti. The first and second violins must leap to a high position on their first strings and bow a double stop with this high note and the open second string. Viola must find two stopped tones for the double stop. Cello stops two strings and bows a triple-stop, including the open A string; the player must remember a direction given in an identical situation at the beginning of the movement, *non arpeg. possible.*

241

Double basses are double-stopped also; and piano, bass drum, and harp do their best to add punch to the ensemble. The only doubling possible of harp strings is E-F♭, for A can be obtained only on the A string. The effect of this doubling on the ensemble is certainly negligible, but it is not like Stravinsky to pass up an opportunity to take advantage of even so slight a reinforcement of the *tutti* when doing so utilizes an individual instrumental oddity.

Brilliant forceful trumpets in octaves follow the *tutti* stroke, and these two measures are repeated without change. The second violin and viola hop around from chord tone to chord tone. First trombone joins second trumpet. In the next measure the motive is further intensified: four horns double first trombone, and second trumpet joins first trumpet at the unison. The first violin also doubles first trumpet and is instructed to play octave double-stops on the first two tones. Stravinsky, aware of the players' habit of dividing rather than double-stopping, specifies *non Div.*

The chord of B major is then hammered out by the *tutti*. The strings are *pizzicato* this time; but the effect is not very different, for the chord is dominated by the wind instruments. The A in timpani is reminiscent of earlier practice, for it would appear that here, where timpani is certainly required, the pretuned wrong note is tolerated. In actuality the timpanist could have arranged for a B to be available, and the A is probably retained as a pedal point. If so, it is difficult to understand why no other bass instrument is concerned with it.

The use of the piano as a percussion instrument is illustrated in the passage that follows. Here the player whangs away at the keyboard almost as if his arms were drumsticks.

The flute plays the entire phrase, and in the score appears at first glance to be the dominant instrument. In sound, however, the effect is one of busy general chatter, and piccolo, xylophone, piano, harp, and first violin take conspicuous parts in the proceedings.

Second violins and viola accompany with *pizzicato* descending fifths, maintaining the urgency of rhythmic motion.

The fairly modern device of doubling melodic lines, not only at the octave (the second harmonic), but also at the twelfth (the third harmonic) occurs in the second half of this passage. Cello, lower viola, lower second violin, and second horn sound the fundamentals. Upper viola and upper second violin sound the second harmonics, and first violin and first clarinet the third harmonics, twelve scale steps above the fundamentals. The device is also applied to the upper melody, in harp and piano.

The three heavy blows struck in the following measure feature quadruple-stops in violins and viola and triple-stops in cello, all *pizzicato*.

Trombones and tuba are omitted, probably because they are busy fitting mutes or are already muted and are therefore unsuitable. Horns are assigned to the pitches previously sounded by the first and second trombones, and the first and second bassoons, inexplicably omitted earlier, help to replace the low brass.

It is doubtful that the movement of the flute, from E to A and back to E, has any appreciable effect; but again, it is typical of Stravinsky to keep something going on whenever possible.

In the last measure of the quotation, muted trombones, doubled by first and second oboes, and muted bass trombone and tuba, doubled by clarinets, have a syncopated echo of the *tutti*. The combination of the penetrating tones of the low register oboes and the acrid-sounding muted brass produces a sharp-edged, brittle effect.

Hindemith

THIRD MOVEMENT

Mathis der Maler

EXAMPLE 55

247

248

250

THIS COMPOSITION, of which measures 1-28 of the finale are reprinted here, is its composer's best-known work and is one of the most frequently performed contemporary symphonies. Unlike the German symphonies of the classical tradition, from which Paul Hindemith is descended, *Mathis der Maler* is a program symphony. In other respects it conforms to the classical ideals of seriousness of purpose, spaciousness of form, and coherency of development.

The orchestra is more clearly used as a vehicle for the expression of abstract musical ideas in this work than for an even incidental display of largely instrumentally inspired effects. This is not to imply that Hindemith shows any lack of scoring skill, but that the technic of orchestration is a secondary concern of the composer, as it is and has been to most serious writers of music. The splendors of the modern orchestra have clouded the judgment of many an orchestrator, but the uncompromising discipline to which all great composers must subject themselves militates against excess of any kind.

The opening of the final movement, subtitled "The Temptation of Saint Anthony," is intensely dramatic and graphically portrays the pangs that the soul-searching Saint endured.

It opens with unison violins, violas, and cellos in a carefully and clearly notated recitative-like passage. As it increases in fervor, oboes and clarinets are added as reinforcement. They do not double the string parts exactly, because this would require the simultaneous entrance of the four unison woodwinds, an unwarranted abrupt change of texture. Instead, first oboe and first clarinet double first and second violin, and second oboe and second clarinet join viola and cello as they diverge from the other strings.

The trills in strings increase the excitement, and the *crescendo* builds up to a thunderbolt from the *tutti.*

The distribution of instruments in measures 5 and 6 should be compared with that of the similar accents in the *Firebird* excerpt. The difference in sound between the two is largely due to the arrangement of horns, trombones, and tuba. The Hindemith is more heavily weighted, as befits the situation.

Timpani, snare drum, and cymbal *tremolandos* taper off the *fortissimo,* and the recitative begins again.

This time only first and second violins are used on the melody, and the violas and cellos are given a few accompanying tones. The C-B♭ and A-D in the viola part are written as double-stops, as are all the double notes in the string parts, for unless the word *divisi* (or its German equivalent, *geteilt*) appears, it is assumed that double-stopping is intended. Hindemith has in other parts of this score indicated divided strings, but no such indication is given here. Most of the double notes in the string parts are not particularly difficult double-stops; but surely the second violin in measures 12, 13, and 14 is not expected to trill two tones at once! Perhaps because he realized that orchestral string players do not pay much attention to the orchestrator's wishes, but divide all but isolated loud chords as a matter of routine, the composer decided that there was no point in cluttering the score with unnecessary markings. Quite reasonable, but consistency of policy would be appreciated.

Flutes, oboes, clarinets, and viola join the melody at the *fermata* in measure 10, and first and second violins are divided in octaves.

The three trombones add great strength to the tones of cello and double bass. From the *fermata* to the crashing chords six measures later, the opening six measures are repeated, transposed to the dominant key and much more strongly scored.

As the second climax is approached, the descending lines are more heavily scored in proportion to the stationary tone of first violin, upper half of second violin, piccolo, first oboe, and first horn. The combined cellos, double basses, trombones, and bassoons can assert themselves clearly over almost any competition.

The climactic chords produce almost the same effect as before, but close inspection of the score will show that some of the instruments are as much as a fifth higher or a fourth lower than in measure 6. The trumpets are noticeably lower, but the horn, trombone, and tuba parts, in spite of the interval of a fifth by which the chords have been transposed, have been arranged to fit into the same strong middle registers which give these declamatory claps of orchestral thunder their solidity.

When the percussionists again succeed in quieting the arena, the recitative is resumed.

The high pitch of energy is lessened and only first violin speaks; and as though it were exhausted by the preceding tension but is still undaunted, the melody is short but positive, and the brass and percussion, like a Greek chorus in sympathy with the protagonist, comment with a mild form of the chords that have punctuated the two preceding orations.

This effect is enhanced as the viola at a lower level of pitch and dynamic, answers the first violin with a statement that ends with a downward turn as opposed to the preceding violin: a sort of question-and-answer. The attentive and responsive chorus of brasses and percussion (cello and double bass also contribute their *pizzicato* string tones to these chords) more quietly underlines the viola pronouncement. Cello deliberates on all the foregoing and leads the orchestra into the 9/8, the finale proper.

The melody is scored for strings spread over three octaves. Viola, alone on the middle octave while the octaves above and below are doubled, is reinforced by both bassoons, who lend their support without obtruding themselves and without distracting from the string tone.

The insistent rhythm of the accompaniment has forms of its own. First oboe and first clarinet, with the same pitches to play, have different rhythmic patterns, and second oboe and second clarinet have even more individualized sequences. Horns and trumpets, after the rhythmic pulse is established, are rotated; and the whole group is employed, with the addition of first trombone as bass, only at the end of the unison string phrase. The old rule of "two woodwinds equal one brass" is illustrated here. First oboe and first clarinet double first trumpet, and second oboe and second clarinet double second trumpet with good effect. The texture is thinned as the cellos alone play the melody, with horns as the accompanists. The third and fourth horns are doubled, for theirs is the moving and significant line.

Subsequent developments in this work deserve an equal amount of attention. The serious orchestrator will profit by a minute perusal of every detail of its structure.

Bartók

THIRD MOVEMENT

Concerto for Orchestra

EXAMPLE 56

257

258

THAT IT IS POSSIBLE TO utilize the widest variety of orchestral combinations and weld them into a unified, compelling, and absolutely convincing musical whole is forcibly demonstrated in this product of Béla Bartók's tragic exile. Hardly any possible combination of instruments is excluded, and every instrument is featured, in keeping with the title.

The piece is so completely orchestral that it is difficult to draw a line between composition and orchestration. For example, octave doubling of melody is common and cannot be mistaken for two-part writing, but the second movement of this concerto features melodies doubled in parallel minor sixths (bassoons), minor thirds (oboes), minor sevenths (clarinets), perfect fifths (flutes), major seconds (muted trumpets), and other intervals in combination with other melodies. The effect is hardly harmonic, and the two lines are in each case played by a pair of identical instruments.

Individual instrumental personalities and idioms are inextricably woven into the structure to an extent that is seldom equaled in a work of similar stature. Bartók has succeeded in giving the fullest play to his orchestral instincts without compromising his greater instinct for composition.

There are few pages of this score that do not illustrate a valuable and interesting aspect of orchestral versatility. The excerpt reproduced here, measures 23-38, is almost a random selection, and only a thorough study of the complete work will prove the remarks made above.

The third movement is labeled "Elegia." It begins quietly and mysteriously with harp *glissandi;* flute and clarinet flicker up and down in approximations of the harp *glissandi* (for much of the way their arpeggios look like harp tunings), in an accompaniment to a peculiarly constricted, troubled oboe melody.

The first page of our quotation begins with the second measure of the passage following the inconclusive end of the oboe solo.

Flutes and clarinets, in a deliberate but hushed manner, play criss-crossed, indistinct arpeggios. These arpeggios are made of the same tones that formed the harp, flute, and clarinet *glissandi* in the preceding section. The first horn is muted, unmuted for two measures, muted again, and again unmuted. Divided violas add only a whisper, for they have been instructed to bow the tremolo *sulla ponticello,* at the point of the bow.

First and second violins, divided into five parts for two measures, imitate the woodwind arpeggios, preserving the aura of mystery. Clarinets then take up the figure. Cello and first horn share a single line in a way that varies its tone color every two measures or so. Clarinets are similarly associated with first and second violins and violas.

The piccolo solo begins as a contracted form of the earlier oboe melody. The blandness of the piccolo tone here intensifies the prevailing mood of remoteness and other worldliness.

First oboe (not all three, as seems to be indicated in the score), English horn, and first horn comment on a fragment of the piccolo line. The highest and lowest tones of the horn statement are doubled in first clarinet and first bassoon, and the strings play *pianissimo* tremolos in a descending series.

Piccolo bleakly ends the passage unaccompanied, in contrast to the outburst of passion that follows.

The first and second violins in octaves with three clarinets doubling the lower octave sound the melody with great intensity. The downward rushing scale is dominated by viola and cello, with added force provided by three oboes in unison with viola. The third oboe is played by the same instrumentalist who played the English horn solo four beats before. The piccolo soloist is expected to change from piccolo to third flute in one and one-half beats. There will be no great loss of tone if he does not manage it, for flutes, even three unison flutes, are not very decisive factors in this register when doubled by three *forte* oboes and strings.

Clarinets, bassoons, and horns sustain the chord spread over three octaves through the third and fourth beats of the measure, as do the lower strings, in tremolo. Rarely used double-stops appear in double bass, completing the close-position harmony in strings from the bass tone E to the viola E three octaves above.

First horn sustains the first note of the cello scale. In this score the unusual procedure of writing first and third horns (the high horns) on the upper line and second and fourth horns (the low horns) on the lower line is followed. It should be noticed that the interlocking of horns described earlier is nevertheless in effect, and the exception lies in the notation of the score, not the assignment of parts.

Trombones and tuba play the chord as a short, heavy accent, which is far less forcibly answered on the fourth beat by flutes and oboes.

Unison harps, marked *fortissimo*, because all their power will be needed if they are to be heard, sound the chord on both the third and fourth beats.

The timpanist, here required to play two drums at once, has an approximate imitation of the rhythm of the first and second violin melody. The cries of the first trumpet sound clearly above the mass of orchestral sound.

FURTHER ANALYSIS

The full score of any orchestral composition with which the student is familiar should be analyzed in the same way as the preceding selections. Any passage of an orchestral work that seems particularly outstanding in performance should be looked up and examined. Familiarity with the style and technic of masters of orchestral music of all periods is the goal. A great deal of experience is required before the sound of a score can be realized through reading, and no opportunity to read and hear simultaneously should be missed.

Selectivity of the material for study is less important than the amount of material studied, but perhaps the symphonies of Mozart, Beethoven, and Brahms, and works of Wagner and Richard Strauss should be studied before less influential compositions are analyzed. In addition to helping the student to acquire orchestral technic, this study will afford him insight into other aspects of musical art and will aid in the development of his general musicianship.

PART THREE

Applied
Technic

10

Introduction

ORCHESTRAL TRANSCRIPTIONS of music originally written for other media, usually the piano, have been common ever since the orchestra became established as the most flexible instrument. There is no better way to learn to score than to translate suitable compositions into the orchestral language, for the novice who does this is able to devote his efforts to purely orchestral problems: the absolutes of musical composition are already provided. A sense of discipline is also acquired, for each composition to be transcribed has an essential character or purpose of its own and imposes limits of expression that must be observed if distortion is to be avoided.

Every solo performer studies each facet of the structure and character of the pieces included in his repertoire before offering them in concert, for his interpretation is valid in direct proportion to his understanding of the work, both intellectually and emotionally. The orchestrator who transcribes a piano piece is, in a sense, interpreting that composition, and has an equal obligation to delve into its every aspect.

Piano music cannot simply be copied, transposed, bowed, and arranged on score paper, for composers of piano music are limited by the spread of the hands over the keyboard and make frequent use of the instrument's powerful built-in harmonics, aided in coloration by the pedals. These technical considerations influence both the sound and the notation. For example, if a very heavy full-chord accent is needed, the best way for the pianist to produce it is to play very low bass tones and very high treble tones with great force. The middle octaves, seemingly silent, are actually important participants in the sound, for all the harmonics of the bass tones are represented by strings that respond audibly, particularly so when the dampers on the strings are raised by use of the sustaining pedal. No such invisible reinforcement is possible in the orchestra; therefore as has been seen in numerous scores, full-chord accents require that the majority of instruments be centered in the middle octaves.

In all cases the *sound* of the music must be the guiding factor, not the notation.

Just as no performer will duplicate in every detail another's conception of gradation of nuance or modifications of tempo, no two orchestrators will produce identical scores. Many faithful and convincing versions of the same work are therefore possible.

Methods of approaching the task may vary also, but a few remarks may be helpful to the beginner. By the time the composition to be scored is thoroughly understood, it is likely that a general plan of instrumental events will have suggested itself. This first impression should be well tested; its instrumental practicality, its stylistic suitability, its contrast versus its continuity, and its adaptability to and reinforcement of the formal design of the piece must be verified.

Actual scoring is best done in short sections, one or two phrases at a time, for the complete ensemble, rather than in long sections for one or two instrumental groups.

Enough score paper to complete the entire project should be prepared with bar lines, clefs, and key signatures before any notes are written; for when work is in progress, it is an aggravating distraction to have to stop and write them in, especially when the key is F♯ major.

The final steps are checking and editing. The score should be mentally read through in tempo, and any omissions, exaggerations, or superfluities marked and subsequently corrected. Every line should be checked for completeness, clarity, and accuracy of notation. Needless to say, it is folly to write a working manuscript score in ink, but if by chance a performance is to be had, it is only courteous to supply a clear inked copy for the conductor.

The scoring projects that follow can give only the beginning of orchestral skill, for good orchestration, like good instrumental performance, is a combination of talent, long experience, and effort. Those, even the very talented, who complete these scores will have gained the beginning of experience; but long experience and applied effort are the responsibility of each individual student.

Schumann

THEME

Symphonic Études, Opus 13

EXAMPLE 57

A MELODY THAT PROMPTED Robert Schumann to write seventeen variations (and publish twelve of them) is our first subject for transcription. Its broad harmonies and rich texture are well within the scope of orchestral expression (many pianistic masterworks are not) and can be effectively scored for a diversity of instrumental combinations.

270

Its form is simple. Phrase 1, measures 1-4, and Phrase 2, measure 5 to the third beat of measure 8, comprise Part I, a period ending in the relative major key. Phrase 3, measures 9-12, is new and leads to a semi-cadence in the tonic key. Phrase 4 is a modified recurrence of Phrase 2; and although a perfect cadence is expected, it ends with another semi-cadence in order to lead to the variation that follows. Since we will not go on to this variation, a tonic chord has been added as an optional ending, to avoid unresolved dissonances.

The form of the piece has been variously labeled as an incipient, or small, three-part song form, an A BA form, and a two-part song. The student is free to use the label that seems best; but he must absorb the sequence of events and believe in their logic.

Texturally rich and dynamically varied, the page shows many pianistic characteristics. The vertical wavy lines in measures 2, 3 and 4 indicate that the pianist should arpeggiate these chords. It is doubtful whether Schumann really felt that these arpeggios are necessary to the musical moment; they may be simply a recognition of the fact that most pianists' hands are too small to stretch these intervals, so that they can play them only by rolling the hand from thumb to little finger. The same effect is obtained, though it is notated differently, on the first beat of measure 8. The intent is obviously to insure fullness of sound by covering as much of the keyboard as possible. The orchestra is able to provide fullness of sound without sacrificing unanimity of rhythm, and no attempt to approximate these arpeggios should be made in the score.

The pedal indications may also be ignored. The sustaining pedal is employed throughout only to help the pianist attain the required *lega-tissimo* and generally to enrich the tone.

Six voices are present in measure 1, five in measure 2, four on the second beat of measure 4, and eight in measure 14. Such variations in texture are typically pianistic and in general result from the limitations of the span of the hands and the attempt to vary tone and texture. There are more graceful ways to vary tone and texture in the orchestra, and careful attention must be given to this aspect of transcription. It is quite possible (and wise) to reduce the piece to four essential voices throughout. Octave doubling and harmonic reinforcements may then be added, but it is not always obvious which tones appear in the piano version merely because a finger happens to be available to play it, which tones are omitted merely because no finger is available to play it, or which chords are enriched by the addition of tones merely for the sake of increased volume. Only attentive listening to the contour and the gradations of nuance of each phrase as played will help in the solution of these riddles.

The string orchestra is best suited to performance of this work, for it can provide the whole range of tone and dynamic with a rich and consistent quality. A five-line score, with cello and double bass on separate

Measure 1 presents a typical problem in the transcription of piano music. Essentially it contains only a melody outlining the tonic triad over the tonic bass; but Schumann has enriched the tone by adding the fifth above the tonic in bass, doubling the melody in the octave below, and completing the triad between the melody and its doubling. The G♯ in the bass enriches the piano tone with its harmonics; but its effect in the orchestra, where richness will be implicit in the upper strings, will be to thicken rather than enrich the texture. The bass part is doubled in octaves elsewhere or is written as a single unsupported line, and it is only in this first measure and its two recurrences that this bass fifth is used. Cello and double bass in octaves on C♯ will provide a clear and satisfying bass. If the G♯ is felt to be necessary, care must be taken to insure that it does not outweigh the true bass tone. This will undoubtedly happen if the cello sounds G♯ against a double-bass C♯. Double-stopping or division of cello is therefore required.

The octave doubling of melody is a more essential element and should be retained, but why is it not continued to at least the third beat of measure 2? Two reasons are possible: (1) that the doubled octave in measure 2 would be very awkward for the performer, and (2) that it would produce a series of close-position chords in the center of the structure, separated from the melody and the bass, and quite likely to emphasize unduly the inner parts. No orchestral awkwardness would result, but the texture would surely be affected if the doubled melody were continued. This is not as distracting in strings as it is on a piano; especially since breadth of harmony is an important aspect of the piece. Therefore, octave doubling of the melody in the second measure is justifiable, and another voice may be added to close the gap between the melody and the inner parts, thus maintaining continuity during the first two measures. The following example shows two possible arrangements of the opening measures.

In measures 3 and 4 the melody descends too low to permit effective doubling and it should be confined to the upper octave. The inner parts must be rearranged to fit the range of the second violin. Tones may simply be added for that instrument, or the alto and tenor parts may be inverted. If the former alternative is adopted, care must be taken that the voice-leading is correct and that Schumann's harmony is unaltered. If the inner voices are inverted, the last two chords will be found unsatisfactory and further revision will be required. Also it will be wise to raise the bass an octave to avoid the wide empty space between bass and lowest inner voice.

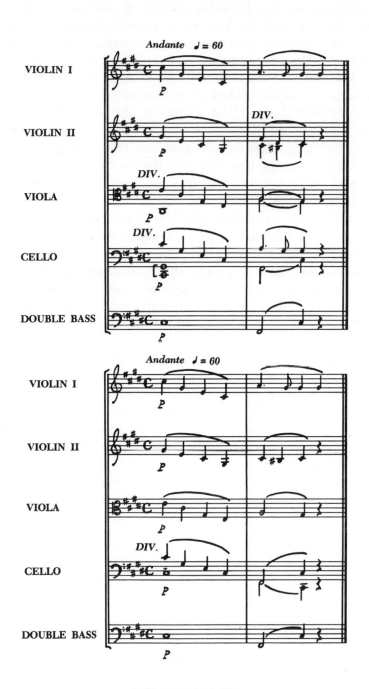

EXAMPLE 58

There should be no noticeable change of texture between the first and second phrases, and the first measure of each should be identically scored. Because of the disposition of upper voices, the bass line is undoubled during this passage because pianistic limitations forbid it. Orchestrally, the bass line is desirable and effective in at least half the cellos and doubled in the octave below in double basses.

Measures 6 and 7 should be examined carefully, for much pianistic reinforcement is present. The effect of expanded harmonic texture must be retained, but each instrumental part must be a logical and melodic line. The change from the high point of the *crescendo* to the sudden and dramatic *piano* in measure 7 offers a convenient opportunity for any necessary redeployment of forces.

The third phrase (including the last three eighth-notes of measure 8) features a more subdued texture, straightforward four-voice writing. To emphasize the reduction of weight, the double basses may be omitted. The bass line under the trill should under no circumstances be doubled, for the two lower voices must be as evenly weighted as possible. Double bass may re-enter at the *sforzando* in measure 12 with a *pizzicato* G♯, returning to use of the bow (*arco*) at the three eighth-notes which lead to the fourth phrase.

No new situations arise in phrase 4, and it should be scored in the manner of phrases 1 and 2.

The bowing must be clearly indicated in the score. Another examination of Grieg's "Ase's Death" may be helpful here. The tempo and dynamic indications must be considered; and at every stage of scoring the *sound* of the orchestra, with reference to the roles of the individual instruments, must be present in the mind's ear.

It is actually quite difficult to make an unplayable and wholly ineffective score of a relatively simple piece like this; but the more care expended upon its technical and musical aspects, the more beautiful it will be.

Beethoven

FIRST MOVEMENT THEME

Sonata, Opus 26

EXAMPLE 59

B. 135.

IN 1802, while he was composing his second symphony, Ludwig van Beethoven published his twelfth sonata for the piano. It was a somewhat experimental work, its four movements being a theme with five variations, a scherzo, a funeral march, and a rollicking rondo. The theme of the first movement is an interesting subject for scoring and it is reproduced here as first published.

Original editions of Beethoven's piano works are notoriously unreliable, and all have been edited, revised, and explained by an army of pianistic authorities of various opinions and degrees of competence. This theme, for example, appears without real phrasing, but with something halfway between phrasing and string bowing. Also, since it was written for the keyboard, the voice-leading is not always clear.

The piece is a three-part song form. Part I, measures 1 to 16, is a double period consisting of four four-measure phrases, the first and third identical to each other (except for the slight modification in measure 9) and the second and fourth identical except at the cadences. Part II is a period of two phrases, the second of which is extended two measures and modulates to a strong cadence in the dominant key. The dominant key becomes the dominant chord and leads to Part III, a recurrence of the last two phrases of Part I.

More important to the orchestrator are the musical content and textures contained within this framework. The first phrase features a melody doubled in octaves. It is accompanied by the bass line, one inner voice, and a constant dominant organ point doubled at the octave. The organ point is not always written in by Beethoven, but its sound is unquestionably present throughout the phrase. The phrase occurs three times in the composition, and the organ point in its first measure is written correctly only once (measure 27). Its absence can be ascribed to carelessness on the part of either Beethoven or his publisher. It is again omitted in the third measure of the phrase (measures 3, 11, and 29), but this time there seems to be a plausible reason. Low-pitched tones a third apart sound thick and muddy on the piano, since it is so rich in overtones. Beethoven omits the low E♭ on the second beat of measure 3 in order to avoid giving undue prominence to an accompanying part. In measure 4, he indicates that the upper octave of the melody is to dominate the lower. The D♭ on the first beat is an appoggiatura that resolves to C. The melody in the lower octave, which, up to this point, has been an exact duplication of the upper octave, omits the appoggiatura and sounds the C on the first beat, creating a sharp dissonance which contributes to the effect of the *sforzando* at that point. It is very likely that the *appoggiatura* in the lower octave was omitted for pianistic reasons. If a pianist were required to play the melody in the lower octave as well as the upper, he could do

278

so only by playing the Db, C, and Bb with his right thumb. This means jumping from the C, thereby accenting the Bb, which would give the lower voice a strength beyond that of the upper, contrary to the composer's intention. No such imbalance is admissible in this first phrase, for it is a quiet, mostly stepwise melody over an almost static harmonic accompaniment of tonic and dominant chords.

The second phrase (measures 5-8, and 13-16) contrasts with the first in marked manner. The melody is no longer doubled in the octave below, and is more angular in its consecutive leaps of fourths and fifths. The bass line is assigned to a register in which we would normally expect to find a tenor part. And the harmonic rhythm is accelerated; in phrase 1 six chord changes occur in four measures, in phrase 2, ten and a modicum of chromaticism is used in contrast with the diatonic I and V chords of phrase 1. In measures 31 and 32 Beethoven combines the elements of the two phrases. The melody and harmony are of the second phrase, but the doubling of the melody in the octave below and the register of the bass are of the first.

Part II, in its first phrase (measures 17-20) is lighter, consisting of a melody doubled at the third below and a single line, not really a bass, as accompaniment. The fact that the harmonic picture is complete because of the presence of three pitches does not alter the fact that there are only two melodic parts here. The second phrase of Part II (measures 21-26) contains the high point of the composition and its climax. Pianistic considerations limit the fullness for which Beethoven obviously strove. His dread of the jumping thumb cost him the doubled melody in measures 23 and 24, and the span of the hands forced him to choose between the melody and the bass as the beneficiary of octave doubling—he could not double both. His decision is interesting: he doubles the melody in measures 21 and 22; but when faced by the imminence of the jumping thumb, he switches to the doubled bass line.

In order to ease the strain on the beginning orchestrator, the conclusions and opinions reached in the above analysis are illustrated in the following version of the work. This is not a condensed orchestral score, but an attempt to depict clearly every detail of the theme as implied in the piano version.

EXAMPLE 60

Set up a ten-line score for two flutes, two oboes, two clarinets in B♭, two bassoons, two horns in F, first violin, second violin, viola, violoncello, and double bass, thirty-four measures long. Add clefs and key signatures on each page and instrument names and time signature on the first page only. Study both written versions of the piece (Examples 59 and 60) and play it or listen to it played on the piano. After every nuance and textural characteristic of the work has been thoroughly digested, its transcription into orchestral tone may be approached.

The first consideration in scoring the work should be the octave melody of the first phrase. Three possibilities exist: predominant upper octave, predominant lower octave, or evenly weighted octaves. The first impulse is, as always, to give the melody to the first violins. The lower octave can then be given, if the upper octave is to dominate, to a bassoon. This was a favorite combination of classical orchestrators and is well suited to the present situation, since internal evidence indicates that Beethoven intended the upper octave to prevail. If the lower octave were preferred, the cellos would be chosen, probably best doubled by bassoon or horn, or both. If the cellos are used on the melody, the second bassoon or the second horn (or both, again) would be needed to replace them on the bass line an octave above the double bass. If the weight of the melody is to be evenly divided between the two octaves, violas and first bassoon are the logical choices. (Violas alone are not always enough to equal the violins in melodic situations.) The cello tone is so rich that it is likely to attract the ear more than the first violins above.

If the upper melody is not given to the first violins, the alternatives are all rather special colors. Clarinet and bassoon in octaves are warm-toned and appropriate to the style but may produce an even octave, and other woodwind combinations are too exotic. Flutes are in their lowest, weakest register, oboes are uncomfortably strident, and horns would lend too much earnestness to the placid tune. Winds on the lower octave are even more limited. The reedy low-register clarinet was almost never used as a melodic instrument in the classical era, nor, because of its lack of valves, was the horn. If either of these instruments is given the lower-octave melody, the experienced listener will have the impression that they are substituting for a missing or incompetent bassoon or string section.

Assuming then, that the melody is given to the first violins and the first bassoon in octaves, the accompaniment must be assigned to the remaining available instruments. The natural bass of the orchestra is the octave combination of cello and double bass, and there is no adequate substitute for them here. Beethoven's bass line is perfectly suited to them during this first phrase. The octave organ point E♭ is a natural horn part.

In Beethoven's day the part would have been written for two horns in Eb as follows:

HORNS I and II
in Eb

p

EXAMPLE 61

Even though we now write exclusively for horns in F, this type of stable and diatonic horn part should be approximated in all orchestral arrangements of works, such as this one, whose style is so obviously of the prevalve period. Even when valves did become standard equipment, many orchestrators continued to write their parts as though they were still limited to the tones of one harmonic series.

If desired, the violas, *divisi*, may double the horns. Their tone will add unity to the structure. If the second violins are given the line beginning on middle C, the whole structure will be represented in the strings. Considering the flavor and atmosphere of the phrase, this is a desirable state of affairs.

The contrasting texture of the second phrase, as described above, requires a change of orchestral tone. Abruptness should be avoided, however, for the role of Phrase 2 as a logical answer to Phrase 1 must not be obscured. The first violin continuing the melody will preserve unity, as will the cellos on the bass line. The second violin and viola are natural and effective choices for the two inner lines. Brightness, fully justified by the more complex structure, may be obtained by the addition of the first flute doubling the first violin in the octave above. If more richness is desired, each string part may be doubled at the unison. First oboe will sharpen the tone of the melody in first violin. First and second clarinets may double second violin and viola, and, to balance the phrase in the woodwind section, the first bassoon may join in on the cello part. Double basses must be omitted in the second phrase, for their presence would eliminate the effect of change of register so obviously intended by Beethoven. The second flute may double either of the two inner parts in the upper octave. The lower of the two is better here, for the two flutes will then be separated. Since they are alone in this register, a better balance is achieved if they are not lumped together.

The repetition of the period should be a repetition of the scoring. The cellos and basses in measures 15 and 16 are best if written one octave higher than the piano bass. In such a short work it is not wise to sacrifice the compactness and explicitness of the musical thought by fussy over-orchestration. In a longer work, when later development of opening orchestral contrast is possible, it is common to change the scoring in repeated periods. The slow movement of Beethoven's Second Symphony, similar in mood and texture to the present subject of study, is a good example. Repeated scoring of repeated periods in small forms may be seen in Brahms' orchestral *Variations on a Theme of Haydn.*

The first four measures in Part II of this composition, beginning in measure 16, offer an opportunity to apply one of the favored orchestral devices of Classical composers—the octave doubling of pairs of woodwinds. Here, because of the high-pitched accompaniment, only two octaves are usable. Two oboes or two clarinets doubled in the octave above by two flutes are perfectly suited to this passage. First and second violins may double the clarinets or oboes if desired, but here the woodwinds are quite sufficient and highly effective alone. The accompanying line, punctuated as it is with typically Beethovian dynamics, must be given to instruments that will preserve its character and yet not outweigh the woodwind melody. The versatile cellos can do this. First horn can help with the *sforzandos.* The two may be combined as follows:

EXAMPLE 62

The first bassoon may double the cellos at the unison.

The next phrase (beginning in measure 21) calls for a *tutti,* for it contains the high point of the piece. First and second violins in octaves, doubled at the unison by oboes or clarinets or a mixture of one of each, should play the melody. The first flute is best doubling the first violin in the upper octave, and the second flute may again be given a line made of inner voices. Clarinets, oboes, and violas will take their parts from the piano version in the original register, maintaining respect for the rules of

284

voice progression. An idiomatic part for the horns may be devised, for instance, one of the following:

EXAMPLE 63

Every tone used in these manufactured horn parts is harmonically correct, but their contrapuntal motion is completely dependent upon Beethoven's original lines. No new countermelody has been devised, and no new harmonic effect has been added. Horns are natural recipients of this treatment, for their tone quality is required for the fullness called for here, but none of the extant parts seems suitable to them. The frequent use of open fifths and octaves between two horns in melodic or accompanying passages that may double any of the tones already present is an easy way to approximate the classical style of writing horn parts. Although being able to approximate classical horn writing may be considered an accomplishment as valuable as competence in phrenology, the importance of the principle of consistency of style is emphasized by such experiments.

The first phrase (as it appears in measures 9-12) recurs without modification in measures 27-30. It should be scored as it was in its first appearance, for the form of the piece is thereby underlined, and the phenomenon of return is emphasized. If a hint of contrast or greater intensity is desired, or a tapering off of the *tutti* of the preceding phrase is felt to be needed, a fragment of the melody may be given to the first horn.

EXAMPLE 64

It will not upset the balance or disturb the sense of return, and will help maintain continuity while providing contrast.

Measures 30 and 31, as previously mentioned, combine elements of both the first and second phrase. The presence of all instruments used in earlier occurrences of these two measures would thus seem to be justified. A *tutti* is also implied because of the concluding and final, and relatively strong, character of the passage.

As always, let us first assign the written parts. First violin, second violin, viola, and cello are inevitable for the four lines of the piano version. In order to preserve a vestige of the original flavor of the music it may be best to omit the double basses, or to give them only an eighth-note F on the first beat of measure 30.

Oboes and clarinets may reinforce the strings in various ways. Second oboe, first clarinet, or both may double first violin. The second violin may be doubled by the second clarinet, but not by the second oboe because of the range. Second oboe may be given one of the inner parts of measures 5 and 6. Horns fit best on the most static part, and will be effective if the second horn doubles viola at the unison and first horn doubles second horn in the octave above. If this arrangement is used, the second oboe should play the upper of the two inner voices rather than double the first horn. Second bassoon should double cello. First bassoon could double viola, but since the horns are strongly there already, it is probably wiser to double the melody in unison with the second violins. Flutes simply repeat their measures 5 and 6.

Composers deal with the classical curtsey and bow cadence, illustrated in the final two measures of this composition, in two ways. Either all instruments take part; or else the strings dominate. A *diminuendo* is certainly implied here—it is marked *piano* by the composer—so a minimum of sound is certainly in order and strings alone will suffice (with cellos and double basses again written an octave above the piano bass). On the other hand, it is well to bring the whole orchestra to the point of relaxation, and a *tutti* can be as soft as one may desire. There are possibilities other than either strings alone or full orchestral participation to be considered. Taste and technic should provide a satisfactory conclusion to this piece without further advice.

Thanksgiving Song

A PIANO ARRANGEMENT of a much loved folksong is our next subject for study. It has been scored before, and it is possible that this version is a reduction of an orchestral score. It contains pianistic devices that are commonly used to imitate orchestral effects and will therefore be a valuable exercise in translating pianistic pretentiousness into the less strained orchestral medium.

EXAMPLE 65

Let us assume that the piece is to be included in a "pops" Thanksgiving concert. We ought then to include the complete orchestral personnel and write a straightforward and full-bodied score.

Although the piece is not a product of an identifiable master of musical composition, it is not to be patronized. Our orchestra will be called upon to present a song that is essentially vocal, but the orchestral medium, versatile as it is, can and must be ready to give voice to any musical thought. The instruments to be used are piccolo, two flutes, two oboes and English horn, two clarinets in A and bass clarinet, two bassoons and contra-bassoon, four horns in F, three trumpets in Bb (or C, if preferred), three trombones and tuba, timpani in D, A, and G, cymbals, harp, and the usual strings.

The form of the work is simple. It is obvious that the song and its five-measure introduction is to be heard twice, first rather quietly, and second in as much fullness as can be commandeered. The last nine measures (codetta) must be as hair-raising as possible.

The introduction (measures 1 to 4) must be reduced to four voices, which are scored for strings. The abandonment of the low D in measure 1 is due to the limitation of the pianist's hand, and may or may not be included in the orchestration. Double basses may play a half-note D and then rest, or their D may be sustained with that of the cellos. The strings may be reinforced by clarinets and bassoons. Second clarinet and second violin may be in unison with their principals in measure 1, or enter in measure 2. The tied-over D is only a pianistic convenience.

The end of measure 3 and measures 4 and 5 require additional instruments. Reinforcement of cadences is common, and horns easily perform that function here.

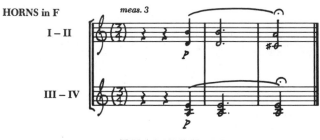

EXAMPLE 66

The abruptness of this entrance of the horns can be eliminated by doubling the second and fourth horns on the cello D from measure 1 on.

A final decorative touch which may be added to the introduction is a quiet timpani roll. The cut-off will be given by the conductor, therefore there need be no special concern for the notation.

The song itself, from the third beat of measure 5 to the first beat of measure 21, should, as in the introduction, be scored for four string parts. Double basses doubling the cello bass line add richness and depth. Woodwinds and horns should not be absent, however, for strings alone would not prepare the listener for the following *tutti*. Clarinets and bassoons may double each string part, or they may be given simplified versions of the harmonic background.

EXAMPLE 67

Variety may be provided by the application of a procedure used in the previously treated Beethoven Sonata, Opus 26: the first horn may add its tone color to a melodic passage made of tones already present in other parts. The horn part need not strictly observe the rules of harmony (voice-leading and permissible doubling), but it must be melodic and must not extend below the bass or above the soprano parts. It need not now be limited to an imitation of hand-horn technic, as was necessary in the Beethoven but an essentially vocal and diatonic flavor should be retained.

A few possibilities are offered:

EXAMPLE 68

Only one of these phrases (2, 3, and 4) should include a horn part; or, if the horn is used in measures 9 through 13, it should be absent at least until measure 17, where, if it is used at all, it should appear in conjunction with another instrument or two whose qualities will dispel any feeling of sameness. Flutes would be pleasant, but they should not be very high, active, or melodic, since their presence is sought only for variety of tone color. Something as simple and unobtrusive as this would suffice:

EXAMPLE 69

The flutes will be clearly heard at their entrance, where they will relieve the obviousness of the horn re-entrance, and will then retire as they descend to a point where they provide little more than atmosphere. Oboes could be used instead of flutes, but their tone quality would be more piercing, nor would they recede as do the flutes.

If the suggestions given above are followed, the score at this point (measure 18) will include first violins and first clarinet, second violin and second clarinet, violas and first bassoon, first horn and first and second flutes, in addition to cello and double bass and possibly second bassoon. This is a rather full score; but as we approach the cadence, the second occurrence of the introduction, and the powerful return of the song, a bit of a suggestion of the coming enlargement may be permissible.

If a timpani roll was a part of the introduction at the beginning, it must be used also in measures 21-26. A good way to anticipate the tone of what follows is to employ the timpani as follows:

EXAMPLE 70

This also provides a valuable element of continuity through the end of the song and the interlude to the restatement of the song. The timpanist's perfectly controlled and gradual *crescendo* will supply a note of drama as it explodes on the first beat of measure 27.

Another horn or two may be added in measures 18, 19, or 20 if even more weight at the cadence is desired.

The introduction, now an interlude, must be much more heavily scored than in its first appearance. Richness of string tone can be obtained by doubling the first violins and cellos in octaves in measures 21 or 22 to 26. If the cellos are used this way, attention must be given to the bass line. Second and fourth horns are now even more fitting than before. The double basses should not be omitted this time; and the combination of double basses, horns, and timpani will provide an ample bass without the cello. The second bassoon, which has doubled the bass line up to now, should not be discontinued, and the bass clarinet, idle thus far, may help out also. (The contra-bassoon is not yet needed, for the texture is not yet thick enough to require that the double basses be reinforced at the unison.)

Violas may be effectively divided to play the two lines in the upper part of the bass clef. They do not lose their solidity when divided and will help maintain the richness of the string tone. The second violin belongs on the inner voice in the treble clef, and should be continued through measure 23. The string parts may then appear as follows:

EXAMPLE 71

Replacing cello in the octave above double bass are second and fourth horns, bass clarinet, second bassoon, and timpani. First clarinet and first bassoon, which have doubled first violin and viola up to now, may be relieved of this duty, for more incisive colors are now required. They, and the second clarinet, may be distributed among the string parts in whatever fashion seems advisable. First oboe doubling first violin will add a sharp edge to the string tone, and second oboe may do the same for the second violin. The first flute doubling the first violin in the octave above, and second flute adding duplicating tones located above first violin and below first flute will add to the spaciousness of the sound. The double-reediness of oboes doubling violins will be aided and abetted if English horn and first bassoon reinforce the divided violas.

If all suggestions have been followed, this interlude is now more fully scored than many familiar classical works. It has been necessary to establish a relatively high level of tone in order to preserve an association with the remainder of the piece. It would be, in such a squarely designed composition of uncomplicated directness of purpose, discouragingly tasteless to use exotic-sounding solo instruments or unusual combinations. Even if the unsupported strings were to be used in measures 6 to 20, the effect would be one of strangeness. The homogenous quality of the brass choir would be most attractive, or a rather precious combination of woodwinds and horns could be used; but in either case the affinity with the full orchestral *tutti* would be lost. In a longer orchestral composition, these and other far more subtle effects are commonplace; but in the present situation any solitary or group soloing is a violation of the style.

A glance at measures 27 and following shows that they cannot be reduced to four parts. They consist of a melody in octaves, a bass line in octaves, an arpeggiated accompanying figure, and filled-in harmonic tones. All these elements have been made available to the two hands of the pianist. The melody can be played by the right thumb and fourth or fifth fingers, leaving the second and third finger to whatever harmonic filling they can manage. The left hand is obliged to cope with the bass and the arpeggios. With the help of the sustaining pedal, this is fairly easy; but when the bass moves on the second and third beats, the arpeggio is sacrificed. The orchestra is not hampered by these pianistic shortcomings, however, and can do full justice to each of these elements. The arpeggios can be made of complete chords, the harmonic fill-ins can (and must) be spread over a wider area, and the melody and bass can be given all the sonority they require.

A more objective version of measures 27 and 28 is:

MELODY

HARMONIC FILL–INS

ARPEGGIO

BASS

E X A M P L E   7 2

Before this section is scored, a clarification of the structure, such as that illustrated, should be made for measures 27 to 41. It should be written out unless the orchestrator is able mentally to conceive and retain a similarly complete picture of events.

Each element must be adequately represented throughout, and a typical plan would be to assign the melody to the first and second violins in octaves and the bass to cello and double bass. The violas are probably best given the arpeggio figure *divisi*, playing the lower two tones (or any two of the three-tone version). This will provide the harmonic support in strings, not otherwise available when first and second violins are doubled on the melody. They may, however, double the second violin melody, leaving all accompaniment to the winds.

First and second clarinets and bass clarinet can be given the three-part arpeggiated chords. English horn and bassoons may double the clarinets. Contra-bassoon doubles double bass. First and second oboes lend their tones to reinforce the first and second violins, but flutes would be lost if used here.

Remember the distribution of tones in the beautifully balanced *tutti* in Tchaikovsky's "Trepak," and give attention to the spacing in the upper octave, where only piccolo and flutes can be used.

The first flute cannot double first violin an octave above because of range, but piccolo can. Flutes filling in the harmony between first violin and piccolo would violate the principle of open spacing in the extreme registers. The best arrangement rather buries the second flute, but any other would tend to either bury both flutes, or clutter up the top octave. The intervals of a fourth or fifth do not contradict the openness of the chord.

EXAMPLE 73

The brass instruments will be very conspicuous and their parts should be prepared with care.

The key is awkward for the trumpets. If the first trumpet is given the melody doubling the second violin (the upper octave is too high), the second and third trumpets are forced into their lower registers, and the brilliance of the trumpet tone is minimized. We can fall back upon the classical practice of writing fairly static supporting trumpet parts, and we can reaffirm the authenticity of the filling-in horn part Example 68 suggested for measure 9 as follows:

EXAMPLE 74

If the first trumpet were to be asked to play the melody for the first four measures followed by the descending scale, a most unbrasslike leap of a major tenth would be required in measure 30. The effect would be awkward and strained if not disastrous.

The trombones could drown out the majority of their colleagues, and even taking into consideration the discretion invariably used by trombone players, their parts must be written in the knowledge that they will be clearly heard. It is possible to give either the first or second trombone the melody; but doing so will very likely focus the attention of the listener on its register to the detriment of the balance established by the careful distribution of the other instruments. A far more common practice is to give them both organ-like harmonic fill-ins. The third trombone (bass trombone) may double cello, or complete the three-part harmony.

EXAMPLE 75

The part for the tuba requires no discussion. Anything other than the fundamental bass would be grotesque.

The horn section can be used in more than one way here, but only in supporting roles. Their usual area of operation is occupied by the trombones, but the horns may be given a slightly more melodic version of the trombone part.

EXAMPLE 76

They might also be used to support the arpeggio. If so, the part could be passed back and forth between the two pairs of horns, which avoids the chance of overworking either.

EXAMPLE 77

297

Timpani and cymbals are valuable in climactic peaks, and it is wiser to omit them during this song. Their effectiveness is much lessened if they are overused, and the inexperienced orchestrator should beware of the temptation to include timpani wherever possible in loud passages. It is better to write no percussion parts until the score is completed in all other respects and then decide on their roles after a mental reading in tempo, for it will then be seen (or heard) just where these instruments will help the ensemble.

The harp, of course, inherits the arpeggio figure and can conveniently manage an expanded version of it and the bass line.

EXAMPLE 78

As the cadence approaches, the distribution of the instruments should be reviewed, for measure 42 must be very brilliantly scored and measure 41 must lead into it without abruptness. Brass instruments should emerge; a simple adjustment in trumpets and trombones will suffice. The first trumpet should not reach the high A (written) until measure 41, and the trumpeter can be given a bit of a flourish as he finally climbs to the upper octave melody.

EXAMPLE 79

The first trombone may double the first trumpet an octave below, and the tonic chord in brass in measure 42 will be solidly arranged as follows:

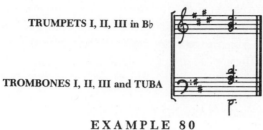

TRUMPETS I, II, III in B♭

TROMBONES I, II, III and TUBA

EXAMPLE 80

For added intensity, first and second violins can leap the octave into measure 42 and use tremolo bowing.

VIOLIN I

VIOLIN II

EXAMPLE 81

The violas may double the violins, or, if they have been playing the arpeggio, continue with it. Horns may either join the other brasses in the sustained chord or reinforce the arpeggio. If additional weight on the arpeggio is felt to be needed, the cellos may combine it with the bass line; their parts would then look similar to the lower staff of the harp part. Double basses should continue with the unadorned bass line, as should tuba and contra-bassoon.

If the arpeggio figure is felt to warrant a dominant role, it can be doubled in the upper octave in piccolo, flutes, and oboes.

The chord in measures 46-47 should be spread as illustrated in Example 82, and sustained for two measures and one beat. The pianistic tremolo is only a means of sustaining the level of volume. It need not be reflected in the orchestra except in the tremolo bowing of the upper strings.

EXAMPLE 82

The bass part in these measures should be given to every instrument capable of playing it in either of the two written octaves.

The low rumble in measures 48 and 49 is an obvious timpani roll. The last two measures should include every instrument capable of playing a strong D in one of the written octaves. This excludes only piccolo and flutes; although the flutes may be included for the sake of togetherness, even though they will not be heard.

It remains now only to add the timpani and cymbals to the last half of the work.

Typical percussion parts include many measures of silence; and scant as these parts are, they include more activity in this piece than those in many a longer work. The complete parts are given to illustrate this point.

EXAMPLE 83

In conclusion it may be said that it is quite possible to score a *tutti* like this more simply. Many similar choral-style works are arranged in four parts with a proper balance of tone maintained between them. Octave doublings are the only addition to the vocal arrangement except for an occasional adjustment to instrumental limitations of range. It is more effective, however, to utilize the individual characteristics of instruments, even very slightly, as here. The suggested horn and trumpet parts are effective not only because they are harmonically and melodically appropriate to the style, but also because they are typical horn and trumpet music. Similar opportunities for idiomatic use of the instruments should be sought in every scoring project, for this use is a most valuable orchestral resource.

Bach

FUGUE XVII

The Well-Tempered Clavier, Book 2

THE MUSIC OF Johann Sebastian Bach is apparently indestructible. No other composer has had his work subjected to more editing, editorializing, revision, transcription, rearrangement, and arbitrary interpretation; but the utter conviction of style, consummate mastery of technic, and untrammeled freedom of expression of the original compositions shines through undimmed. Our present scoring project, therefore, is not without precedent and may be undertaken without fear of desecrating a masterpiece.

The fugue at hand is one of forty-eight written to demonstrate the fact that a keyboard instrument (clavier) could be tuned to the tempered scale so that it could satisfactorily cope with any and all tonalities. The first twenty-four Preludes and Fugues, one in each major and minor key, were completed in 1722; the second group was completed about twenty years later. As are a number of other pieces in the second volume, the Ab fugue is a revision of an earlier work, an organ composition in F major.

Fugue is more a matter of style and technic than of form. The diversity of inward and outward character that Bach exhibited in his hundreds of fugal compositions is a subject for exhaustive study in itself, and it must be borne in mind that the analysis of this composition is an analysis of this composition only.

There are five recurrent thematic elements in the Ab fugue.

EXAMPLE 84

The first (a) is the most impressive, for it contains a variety of leaps, steps, and rhythmic patterns. It is the subject, and occurs more frequently than any other melodic member. The answers are tonal; that is to say, when the subject appears in the dominant key as response to a preceding statement in the tonic, the first tone, which would become the fifth of the dominant if truly transposed, thus going out of the key of A♭ becomes the fourth of the dominant: the tonic note of the principal key.

The parentheses that mark off the first and the last three tones of the second short melody (b) isolate the descending chromatic scale that is its characteristic feature. The first eighth-note is often omitted in subsequent appearances, and the last three cadential tones are sometimes modified for harmonic reasons. This scale accompanies the subject in all occurrences save three and is clearly defined and conspicuous enough to be called the countersubject.

The third thematic element (c) is derived directly from the countersubject. Its first four tones duplicate, in different rhythm, the first four tones of the countersubject and are followed by a descending scale.

A fourth motive (d) is reminiscent of the opening of the subject, and the fifth figure (e) is without any semblance of contrast and seems to be a modified form of the sixteenth-note figure that ends the subject. Its motive makes its first appearance as a free counterpoint in measure 5; (c) and (e) modulate up a fourth, and the tonality of (d) is rather ambiguous. These three tunes always appear concurrently and as contrast to preceding and following statements of the subject and countersubject. They thus perform the function of an episode, and will hereafter be referred to as episode motives (EM) 1, 2, and 3.

Many other attractive melodic phrases occur, usually in association with the subject, but they are not restated and take no essential part in the over-all design. A fundamental requirement of fugal style is that all voices must be melodic, and such nonthematic melodies are called "free counterpoints."

This modest amount of melodic material is manipulated by Bach with enough skill and imagination to give rise to a coherent and fully developed three-part form.

The design may be represented as follows: (The reason for the fractional measures is that contrapuntal melodies almost invariably begin on weak beats and end on strong beats. "Meas. 1-15 5/8" is clear enough and simpler to read and write than "Meas. 1 to the eighth-note on the third beat of meas. 16." It will be understood that each section begins immediately after the eighth- or sixteenth-note on which the preceding section ends.)

Part I (meas. 1-15 5/8); exposition.
  A 1 (meas. 1-9 1/16): entrance of the voices, subject, and counter-subject.

B 1 (to meas. 12 5/8): episode.

A 1 (to meas. 16 5/8): subject and countersubject (one statement) extended to cadence in relative key.

Part II (to meas. 40 1/16): development, or counterexposition.

A 2 (to meas. 26 9/16): subject and countersubject.

B 2 (to meas. 31 1/8): episode.

A 2 (to meas. 40 1/16): subject and countersubject.

Part III (to meas. 50): recapitulation and coda.

A 3 subject and countersubject, transition, and coda.

A few details of the inner structure of these subdivisions will be discussed when their instrumentation is under consideration.

Part II is an expanded version of Part I. Part III is a short but powerful reaffirmation of the subject in the tonic key. The form of part I (A, B, short A) is a miniature of the form of the whole fugue (I, II, short III) and reveals a facet of Bach's genius, the possibly half-conscious ability to endow even minor aspects of his work with form and definitive character.

Most fugues make use of a variety of contrapuntal devices—augmentation, diminution, inversion, stretto, and modified versions of thematic material, singly and in various combinations. This one, however, except for one stretto, rather puny when judged by Bach's usual standard, is devoted entirely to various manifestations of the principle of inversion. In A 1, the subject appears above the countersubject, below it, and below it with a free counterpoint between. B 1 shows the episode motives in two inversions. From top down they appear in the order EM 1, EM 2, EM 3 and inverted to EM 2, EM 1, EM 3. The second A 1 is an example of invertible double counterpoint at the twelfth; the subject is in the tonic key but the countersubject is in the dominant, as it appeared in measures 3 and 4.

The order of keys in the first two appearances of the subject in A 2 is dominant, tonic, an inversion of the tonic, dominant sequence of A 1.

The three episode motives appear in three successive inversions in B 2. The order, again from upper voice to lower, is EM 3, EM 2, EM 1; EM 1, EM 3, EM 2; and EM 2, EM 3, EM 1.

The rhythmically displaced statement of the subject in the bass voice, beginning in measure 37, may be considered to be a rhythmic inversion, for the tones that heretofore have appeared on accented beats are sounded on unaccented beats, and formerly unaccented tones are sounded on the accented parts of the measure. The countersubject in soprano is not rhythmically displaced, but appears in its normal metrical position, just as if the bass subject had not begun one beat too soon.

In A 3 (measure 41) the countersubject, much ornamented but still a descending chromatic scale, appears in the tonic and simultaneously the dominant keys in the alto against the subject in the tonic.

The final example of inversion appears in the sixteenth-note passage which follows the *fermata* in measure 46. The lower part is an almost perfectly mirrored version of the upper.

Many of the free counterpoint passages are, or are derived from, inversions of each other or of the thematic material. Most of the scale lines, interspersed with occasional changes of direction and short leaps, may be traced to their source in the cadence figure of the subject.

The fugue should be studied, played, and listened to; and every detail of its style, structure and personality must be absorbed. The beginning and ending of every thematic line should be marked in the following reproduction of the work. The piece is presented in open score for clarity of line, but the vertical harmonic structure should not be overlooked.

EXAMPLE 85

meas. 9 – 17

meas. 18 – 26

meas. 27 – 35

meas. 36 – 44

This work, in which every tone is melodic, can be scored for almost any combination of instruments. Other Bach fugues have been arranged for everything from string quartet to the fullest symphonic orchestra. The first treatment lends little more than string coloration to the four voices, and the second has too often lapsed into a flamboyant exploitation of the most exotic and bizarre orchestral resources. The object of this project is to portray the composition with a richness and variety of tone far beyond the scope of the piano, but without distorting or experimenting with the intent of the original.

311

Because of the melodic character of each voice and the rapidity of the harmonic rhythm, harp, timpani, and percussion are superfluous and may be omitted from the score. Strings with even an abbreviated woodwind group could do a creditable job, but the dramatic ending justifies the presence of more power. Let us assume an orchestra of paired woodwinds, with secondaries available if needed, four horns, two trumpets, three trombones, tuba, and strings.

Since Bach gave no indications of tempo, phrasing, or dynamics, it is necessary to consider these factors before beginning to score.

The tempo taken by pianists is not usually the best tempo for the orchestra, for the ability to sustain tones and the pure legato available in orchestral instruments make a slower tempo more effective. A metronome speed of $\quarternote = 66$ or less is best.

Phrasing and the location of breathing spots are fairly obvious, for Bach's melody writing is so clear and natural that the lines almost live and breathe by themselves. The ups and downs of volume are also inherent in the lines and texture. This fugue, like most others, is a long *crescendo;* but as in mountain climbing, there are many downgrades on the way up.

Generally speaking, drastic changes of tone color or texture should not occur within individual sections of the work. An instrument to play the opening statement of the subject should not be selected until it is ascertained that the following three statements of the subject and countersubject can be scored without producing any effect of abruptness.

The strings are the logical choice; their suitability will be obvious when other possibilities are considered. If woodwinds are used, there will be no contrasting lighter texture available for the Episode B 1. Woodwind A 1, followed by strings or brass B 1 places the authority and emphasis on B 1, in contradiction of the relative importance of the two sections.

If the first trumpet plays the opening subject, the answer (measure 3) cannot be continued with a brass tone and must be given to a combination of instruments strong enough to match the brilliance of the trumpet. This creates a higher intensity of tone than is permissible at this early stage, for it seriously limits the amount by which the sound of the soprano line can be further intensified in later sections.

Second violin as alto (opening) voice, first violin as soprano, viola as tenor, and octave cello and double bass as bass throughout section A 1 provide a common denominator of tone quality from which the rest of the score may most effectively grow. Variety may be obtained without sacrificing the dominance of string sound by the judicious use of doubling woodwinds. They may double the strings at the unison, only on the subject and not the countersubject or free counterpoints, or only on the countersubject or the chromatic scale of the countersubject. Thus, the string tone can be variously colored, and important thematic elements gently emphasized.

Contrast is called for in the episode (B 1), and woodwinds are the best choice. Their unobtrusive presence in A 1 has prepared the listener for them; this minimizes the danger of abruptness.

As in most woodwind passages the string sound, though no longer dominant, should not be absent. Continuity may be best maintained here by the cello, no longer doubled by the double basses, playing EM 3 along with the first bassoon. EM 2 may be given to the first oboe and EM 1 to first clarinet and first flute in octaves. (The soprano line doubled in the octave above is just as acceptable as bass lines doubled in the octave below.) If EM 1 is given to the first oboe instead of to the first clarinet, and the clarinet then assigned to EM 2, the balance may be poor, for the passage lies in and around the clarinet's relatively weak throat register. The balance may be restored by employing two clarinets in unison on EM 2; the inevitable suggestion of out-of-tuneness and the absence of individuality of expression in unison woodwinds will here be turned to good advantage.

The viola may play the second occurrence of EM 3 (tenor) or the cello may continue. The first bassoon should continue, or first and second bassoon may double cello and viola, respectively. If a need is felt to distinguish between the bass and tenor statements of EM 3, a sequence of bass clarinet and bassoon may be used, but only if the first of these instruments can be used elsewhere.

The three motives of the episode end at different places. The soprano ends EM 2 on the third beat of measure 13, alto ends EM 1 on the first beat of measure 14, and tenor ends EM 3 on the following third beat. The instrumentation of these lines should be the same as that of the first statements: the instruments which played EM 1 in measure 10 should play EM 2 in measure 12, and those which announced EM 2 should continue with EM 1. Any change of color would distract the listener's attention from the inversion of the two motives.

The second A 1 requires emphasis. The relationship of subject and countersubject is new and creates new, more chromatic harmonies. This section also concludes the exposition.

The soprano begins the section with a sequence of the scale of EM 1. First violins should re-enter with this scale (measure 13) doubled in the octave above by one or both flutes, and at the unison in one or two oboes or one oboe and one clarinet.

The countersubject in tenor, in the "wrong" key, is the feature of this section and should be very strongly scored. Viola, two horns (first and third), one or two clarinets and perhaps even a bassoon will not be too much to proclaim its importance. The subject in bass is no less pertinent to the plot, but does not require as much attention. Cello and double bass in octaves, with both bassoons doubling cello, will be sufficient. If the bass clarinet was used before, it may also be included.

A *diminuendo* begins in measure 15, but calls for no decrease in the number of participating instruments. Even the fullest orchestral *tutti* is capable of a dramatic *pianissimo,* and the patchy effect that would result from a contrived attrition in this measure-and-a-half would be far more disturbing than a controlled quieting of the whole company.

If greater richness is desired in this second A 1, the free counterpoint in the soprano may be doubled by the first and second violins in octaves; all other instrumental assignments should remain as described above.

The fact that the structure of part II has the same general outline as that of part I implies that the orchestration should also be similar: dominant or at least conspicuous strings in A 2, woodwinds in B 2, and an effect approaching the *tutti* in the second A 2. A greater diversity of color and a wider range of dynamic level are appropriate during part II, and instruments not previously used may make their appearance.

There are opportunities in orchestral usage for pointing out details of thematic development that usually remain obscure in a piano or quartet performance. One conspicuous example is the use of the figure from the end of the countersubject in A 1. Its leading tone, which resolves up a half-step to the tonic, is chromatically altered and deflects the tonality, postponing the cadence. Its syncopated rhythm is enough to identify it, and it is used independently of the countersubject. It appears in A 2 as follows:

EXAMPLE 86

It finally resolves to a true leading tone, which resolves to the C minor tonic in measure 27.

The second A 2 includes two occurrences of the figure, but the suspensions that have characterized it in A 2 are replaced by positive accents.

EXAMPLE 87

Each of these illustrations is part of a line that must be clearly sounded in its entirety; and the growth of the figure under discussion may be pointed up by adding woodwinds or horn at the unison or the octave above, but not by interrupting the line and substituting a new color. One possibility would be

EXAMPLE 88

This principle may be applied when only diversity of color is desired and no important theme is present. Although it is sometimes effective, it is the surest way to over-orchestration, fussiness, and distortion of the original contrapuntal clarity. One example is given:

Inner voices (alto and tenor) should be doubled in the octave above or below only when such doubling does not create an inversion of parts, which occurs when the original register is so heavily scored that the octave-doubling instrument acts as a reinforced second harmonic. Such would be the case if, in measure 13 and 14, one flute, oboe, or clarinet were to double the countersubject in the octave above.

Another way to attain variety is to sound the original line simultaneously with a simplified version of it. This device (or any other) should not be applied at random, but should be part of a consistent pattern. For example, EM 3 may be scored as follows:

HORN in F

CELLO and
BASSOON

EXAMPLE 89

It is not usually wise to add notes to the works of master composers; but when doing so does not obscure, distort, or unduly exaggerate the original, it may be the only way to obtain the orchestral breadth of tone that seems to be called for. One such instance appears in measures 22 and 23. Here the four voices sound together for the first time, and a relatively high dynamic level is implied. All four horns may take part in an arrangement similar to the following:

HORNS I and II
in F

HORNS III and IV
in F

EXAMPLE 90

In measure 41, where all instruments except those reserved for the bass entrance in measure 42 should take part, a line isolating the tones of the chromatic scale in the countersubject may be added in the register in which a horn or two and perhaps the second trumpet can be used.

meas. 41

EXAMPLE 91

The chords in measure 45 and 46 are written to fit the hand of the keyboard player. They would be rather hollow if scored as written, for the empty middle register at the fermata would be very noticeable. They should be expanded:

EXAMPLE 92

The instrumentation at the *fermata* might be, from top down:

B♭: Violin I, Flute I, (Piccolo)
E♭: Flute II
B♭: Violin II, Trumpet I, Clarinet I
E♭: Trumpet II, Oboe I
D♭: Clarinet II, Oboe II
B♭: Viola, Horn I
E♭: Horn III
D♭: Horn II
B♭: Horn IV

The bass passage in measures 45 and 46 is clear evidence of the composition's origin as an organ piece, for it is typical organ pedal figuration. It is neither easy nor graceful when played on brass instruments, and its effect is not lessened if it is simplified as follows:

(Tuba 8ᵛᵃ lower, sounding in unison with Double-Bass.)

EXAMPLE 93

317

The dissonances of the sixth eighth-note of measure 45 and the second eighth-note of measure 46 are far less disturbing than the harmonic confusion which would result if the accented nonharmonic tones of the original were doubled in the simplified version.

Care must be taken that both the answer, which begins in the third measure before the end, and the countersubject, which accompanies it in the added fifth voice, are clearly heard. Because of the thicker texture, they are often buried in performance. All four horns on the subject and first and second trombones on the countersubject would do the trick. The brassiness of the combination may be softened by doubling each by a woodwind or two.

When a reasonable detailed scoring plan is completed it should be objectively re-examined for the following points:

1. Octave doubling must not distract the listener's attention from the original octave.

2. The subject or answer must never be fragmented. Their instrumentation should be unchanged from the beginning to the end of each statement.

3. Answers to subjects should be orchestrated in a logically answering manner. Most statements are paired: Alto in measure 1 is answered by soprano in measure 3. Tenor in measure 6 is answered by bass in measure 8. Alto in measure 16—really an answer—is followed by tenor in measure 18 —really a subject. Soprano in measure 22 is answered by alto in measure 24. Tenor in measure 32 is answered by soprano in measure 35. Tenor in measure 41 is answered—*stretto*—by bass in measure 42.

4. Pointing up incidental motivic fragments should not detract from the clarity of the line as a whole.

5. Each instrumental part should be melodic at all times.

6. Every phrase or motive should be completed: each tone sounded should be part of an intelligible (to the player) musical thought. The only exception to this principle is the occasional reinforcement of two or three tones as described above; but even here there must be an indication of a purpose such as sequence, imitation, or subplot.

7. The score should show a gradual, though not necessarily regular, increase in volume, diversity and richness of tone color, and intensity of expression.

When all these considerations have been dealt with, the score may be completed. The general check up recommended at the beginning of this section should be done with particular care, for the phrasings, bowings, and dynamic markings are the orchestrator's own and must be clearly and confidently represented if they are to convince conductors and orchestral players of their validity.

This project has been exhaustively discussed because of the complexity of the music and the lack of definitive orchestral precedents. Bach's compositions, more than those of any other composer, are not dependent upon the medium of performance for their effect. This absolute quality subjects any practical realization of his works to criticism, for no performance can bring to actuality the ideal of musical utterance that so many leaders and followers of musicological thought find in unvoiced printed pages of presumably authoritative editions.

The fact that Bach had no modern symphonic orchestra available has been used to justify orchestral transcriptions of his work. It might also be remembered that he had no modern pianoforte, no electrically powered pipe-organ, no singers trained in the *bel canto* tradition, and, according to our most diligent historians, no time to devote to bewailing these shortages. He bravely wrote his music anyway, and the hesitant orchestrator is advised to do the same, here and elsewhere, in spite of officious censure.

Brahms

Variations and Fugue
on a Theme by Handel, Opus 24

Our treatment of this single page from Johannes Brahms' brilliant *Variations and Fugue on a Theme by Handel* will without a doubt be a very far cry from the composer's plans for the work. His utilization in this variation of the percussive quality of the pianoforte makes it an excellent subject for scoring for percussion instruments and for featuring the high-register woodwind instruments.

EXAMPLE 94

Outwardly the form is a simple two-part affair, but the inner structure is more involved. Here again, as in the Ab fugue of Bach, the principle of inversion prevails. There are four motives present, for the sake of convenience here termed A, B, C, and D. Motive A first appears in the upper voice, and B in the middle voice in measures 1 and 2. C and D are the upper and middle voices, respectively, in measures 5 and 6. The reiterated tonics and dominants of the lower part are constant factors which do not figure in the convolutions of the two upper voices.

The sequence of events may best be shown in a diagram.

Measure	1-2	3-4	5-6	7-8	9-10	11-12
Upper Voice	A	B	C	A	D	B
Middle Voice	B	A	D	B	C	A
Lower Voice		Tonic	Dominant	Tonic	Dominant	Tonic

If we first consider the non-percussion instruments to be used, we will see that a large group of players can be dispensed with. No low-pitched instruments are required, except for the lowest voice, which does not extend very low and should not be reinforced with octave doubling. If it is decided to give this lowest part to wind instruments, it must be remembered that breathing places are needed. The best solution is to use two alternating players:

EXAMPLE 95

Clarinets, bassoons, or horns are possible. Either of the woodwinds would be rather weak and easily overshadowed by the activity of the upper voices, but are quite satisfactory if doubled by a string section. Bb trumpet and English horn include these two pitches in their range, but they should not be considered because of the awkward register and the unsuitability of their tone qualities to the task.

Viola, cello, the alternation of viola and cello, or of second violin with either viola or cello are possible for the lower line, alone or doubled by horn or woodwind. The choice should be guided by the realizations that the second violin is best left available to take an upper voice, and that there is little need to use both viola and cello.

Motives A and B require bright-sounding agile instruments capable of a good staccato. Piccolo, high flute, oboe, Eb clarinet, and to a slightly lesser degree, Bb clarinet are well endowed with these characteristics. Violins are of course usable throughout.

323

Motive B is composed of a short figure in sequence, and the tone color may be changed with each occurrence:

EXAMPLE 96

Similar little dialogues may be made a regular part of this motive, but the sequence of instruments must be carefully planned to be sure that no one will be unable to take his turn because of range limitations.

Motive A should be one color throughout each appearance. Its gasping for breath character would be lost if it were broken up like motive B; and also it should contrast with its associate.

Motives C and D are legato. Strings, woodwinds, or both may play. Clarinet is more suitable to D than oboe, and flute would be in its lowest, most easily buried octave. Horn or English horn could play motive D with good effect in measures 9 and 10.

Many charming and novel instrumental versions of this short work can be made. If percussion instruments are employed, the possibilities are multiplied.

The xylophone may be used as one of the participants in motive B, and various other members of the percussion family may be used to support any of the other parts.

A large assortment of these instruments, requiring five or more players, can produce a diversity of effects which might almost render the rest of the orchestra superfluous. The following discussion assumes that it is desirable to have every aspect of the piece represented in a non-melodic percussion instrument.

The tonics and dominants of the lower line should be represented by two deep-toned instruments. A snare drum with snares off may represent B♭ and a tenor drum, a deep, wooden drum without snares, may represent F. Although they sound no pitch, the relationship between their tones will make a more or less acceptable impression of tonality.

Motive A may be sounded in one of a wide variety of ways, from a simple ticking of the rhythmic pattern on a wood block to a more complicated cymbal arrangement. Percussionists are accustomed to seeing a wealth of stage directions in their parts, and the following notation of one possible method of performing motive A would not be considered unusual:

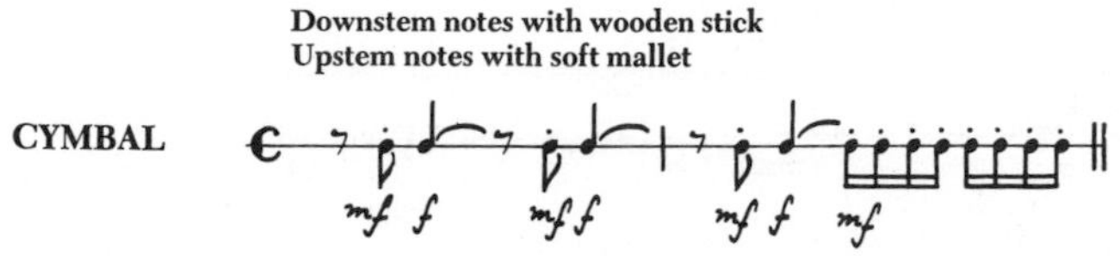

Downstem notes with wooden stick
Upstem notes with soft mallet

CYMBAL

EXAMPLE 97

A combination of instruments may be used, as, for example, a tambourine with the cymbal version shown in Example 97.

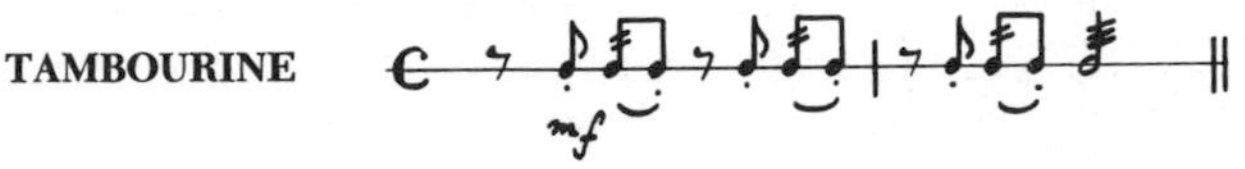

TAMBOURINE

EXAMPLE 98

Motive B calls for staccato-sounding instruments. A group of four is needed: two for the motive when it is in the lower octave and two for the higher octave. Two are needed in each to isolate the short figure at each occurrence. Smaller instruments should be used to represent the higher octave in order to give the impression of higher pitch.

The snare drum is the most brittle instrument and may be used in conjunction with a wood block on the lower octave. The upper may be given to two small, but not identical, temple blocks. All statements of motive B may be given to temple blocks, the short figures being distributed among the five graduated instruments. Strictly speaking, temple blocks are not without pitch, for they are tuned to an approximation of the pentatonic scale. Chinese in origin, these dry and hollow-sounding instruments are rounded blocks of wood, partially hollowed out across the front, and struck with hard padded mallets or wooden sticks.

The relationship between motive A and the lower voice acts to emphasize the rhythm of the lower voice when motive A is silent:

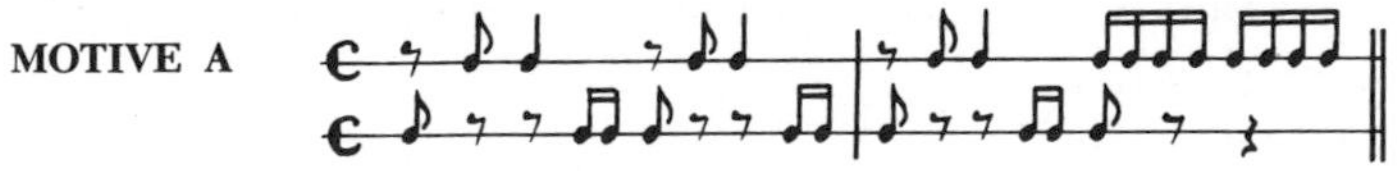

MOTIVE A

EXAMPLE 99

325

Other touches may be added, such as the triangle in the following percussion ensemble version of measures 1, 2, and 3:

EXAMPLE 100

The legato character of motives C and D render them less well suited to percussion, but softness of tone and gently sustained tones where possible will at least help produce an effect less staccato than the preceding section. Two cymbals struck with soft mallets and allowed to ring can approximate a legato:

EXAMPLE 101

The two cymbals must be identical in size and of course may be played by one player. A somewhat similar effect can be had using both mallets on one cymbal.

When temple blocks are struck with rather hard mallets, they are not as dryly percussive as most other percussion; doubled in triangle, they would be quite satisfactory on motive C.

There are obviously many variations possible in scoring for percussion. Discretion and taste are called for, and even more so when percussion instruments are used in combination with other orchestral groups. Decisions on when, how, and how often to use them can be made only with reference to specific musical situations.

It would be profitable to make three versions of the piece under consideration: one for non-percussion instruments, one for percussion ensemble, and one for a mixture of the two. The third version may be the first with percussion added; or it may be one in which the lower voice is given entirely to percussion, varied and enriched as follows:

EXAMPLE 102

or

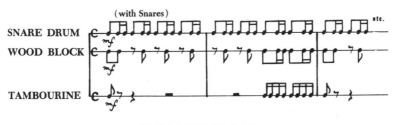

EXAMPLE 103

or any one of a hundred other ways to endow this repetitious rhythmic figure, or any other of the motives, with a more individualized and colorful character.

Study No. 15

ORCHESTRAL MUSIC, by and large, is music conceived in orchestral terms; it is not transcriptions of piano settings. There is no better way to understand style and technic than to study the works of individual composers as they utilize various methods of musical expression. The Brahms style is consistently evident in his orchestral, vocal, piano, organ, and chamber works. So it is with Haydn, Mozart, Beethoven, Schubert, Mendelssohn, Debussy, Ravel, and all others who have attained greatness in a diversity of musical media. (Composers whose personal style lends itself to only one form of expression are usually perceptive enough to recognize that fact, and their contributions to the repertoire of musical masterworks is not diminished by their specialization. Chopin, Verdi, Wagner, and Puccini are proof that musical greatness is not wholly dependent upon versatility.)

The task upon which we now embark is one to which no awareness of the composer's individual style can be applied. The passages that follow were orchestrally conceived, but as always, there is no single correct way to score them.

Analysis of these examples will reveal that five motives are used. Their first appearance occurs in Example 104 as follows:

Motive A: bass clef, measures 1 and 2.
Motive B: treble clef, measures 2, 3, 4, and 5.
Motive C: treble clef, measures 7 and 8.
Motive D: bass clef, measures 10 and 11.
Motive E: the three sixteenth-notes in measure 10.

EXAMPLE 104

Let us assume that this is the beginning of a large orchestral work —a symphony, orchestral concerto, tone poem, or concert overture—and that the composer has seen fit to squander all his thematic ideas on the introduction and construct all subsequent developments on derivations and transformations of these introductory pronouncements.

Motive A seems to be a natural cello-double bass subject, but bassoon or bass clarinet may contribute a touch of woodwind color. Motive B, a single melody in four parts, requires consistency of tone. Modern ears are conditioned to accept mixtures of upper woodwinds as consistent qualities; and almost any arrangement of flutes, oboes, E♭ clarinet, and B♭ or A clarinets is acceptable here. Divided violins, however, are more certain to be even; and if woodwinds are used, care must be taken to ensure that the upper voice predominates.

A third element enters in measure 5, asking for permission to announce motive C in measure 7. It must be scored for the instruments that will rule in measure 7.

Measure 10 is a *tutti*, and motive D in bass can hardly expect to be especially noticeable. A well-balanced ensemble is far more desirable here than singling out any particulars. Motive E, the three sixteenth-notes, is introduced as a reinforcement of the accent and should similarly enrich the ensemble without ostentatiously drawing attention to itself.

From the *subito piano* in measure 12 to the double bar, motives A and D are mentioned with lessening intensity and the orchestra should likewise subside.

Strong stark colors should prevail at the 5/2; and when the "wrong-note" ridden upsweep in measure 21 is scored, all agile members of the orchestral community may be included, for it leads to a stronger *tutti* (Motive E) than has yet been heard. All upper instruments will find a role in the treble-clef parts, and all the baritones and basses will sound the bass-clef line, a vague reminiscence of motive A. The extreme *diminuendo* offers an opportunity for conductors to gesticulate in their most outraged manner, for when measure 28 is reached, the utmost changes to softness and tenderness must have been accomplished.

Motives B and E are then combined, and motive D occurs in the course of the accompanying line. This appearance of motive D should not be scored for the instruments that play the preceding and following sections of the accompanying melody. Motive B is the principal melody; it should be given to an instrument that will sing and realize the melodic quality of the passage. Motive E is helter skelter and sarcastic. It should be distributed among a variety of solo instruments that can demonstrate its lack of concern with concurrent events.

EXAMPLE 105

We abandon this expository section and, skipping many imaginary measures, come to a fragment of development in which motives A, C, D, and E are combined.

The four overlapping recurrences of motive C in the upper parts are accompaniment to the lower parts and may be scored for strings or woodwinds. As the *crescendo* sets in, the strings may be reinforced by gradually added woodwinds or the woodwinds by gradually added strings.

Motives D and E are combined and should be given to instruments that can produce a clear staccato at the required low level of volume.

Motive A in bass is suitable for almost any quiet combination of bass instruments. *Pizzicato* or *arco* cello and double bass, bassoons and bass clarinet, and even trombones and tuba must be considered. The strings would be very subtle, but the melodic function of the line would go almost unnoticed. Woodwinds would be more exotic and draw more attention to the motive. Brasses, even though played very softly, would impart a rather solemn and portentous tone. Since the orchestrator is here thrust into the role of composer, the degree of emphasis to be given to the different motives in this and other passages will be determined by individual taste.

Measure 7 of Example 105 is another forceful *tutti,* this time on motive C. As it fades, the abruptness of the change of dynamic level may be tempered by the use of the more strikingly ear-catching tone colors. Here again personal taste will determine which aspect of the phrase will be made most evident.

The inevitable slow movement may be represented by the following short excerpt, made of motives A and B.

The four-part texture (two lower staves) is a native-born string passage. The lyric character of each line, the plentiful and diversified dynamic indications (whose exaggeration is fully justified), and the obvious need for equality of tone among the four voices add up to a situation to which only the string section can do justice. Winds may be used to reinforce in various ways, but the warm richness of the earnestly singing strings must not be blurred.

Only the gentlest instrumental tones are appropriate to the parts in the upper staff. The mention of motive C at the end may be looked upon as a tremulous and rather wistful woodwind reference to former moments of wind supremacy.

EXAMPLE 106

EXAMPLE 107

This business-like beginning of the final movement requires a compartmentalization of the orchestra into complementary groups. Measures 1 to 7, and 8 to 14, and the passage that begins in measure 15 each require a distinct individuality of instrumental color.

It need hardly be mentioned that motive E is the progenitor of the movement, nor should it be necessary to remark that consistency in the manner of orchestration should be maintained throughout the four contrived quotations of orchestrally-conceived excerpts from this nonexistent large-scale work.

Each of these three phrases should be more brilliantly hued then its predecessor; and the third phrase should be authoritative enough to lead, without undue abruptness, to the obvious *tutti*, motive D, in measure 23.

The *diminuendo* that follows well utilizes the ability of the powerful brass instruments to reduce their brilliance; it also demonstrates that they are quite compatible with the tenuous air of the constricted melodic version of the opening phrase which begins in measure 31. The listeners' attention will be held here only if the melodic instrument employed is capable of playing this rather apprehensive line with an air of sturdy innocence. The instruments that accompany this passage must do so as quietly and delicately as possible.

So ends this venture into a moderate modernity. If a cadential and conclusive ending is desired, the student is encouraged to attempt some homemade music of his own. Mention may be made here of the fact that every orchestrator is at times required to score compositions for which, to state it mildly, he has little sympathy. It is, nevertheless, the orchestrator's mission to treat each project as though it were the most glorious of all musical thought and to score it to the best of his ability. The continued observance of this policy may well be the reason for the dependence, over a wide area of American musical practice, upon arrangers and orchestrators, for their skill can raise the most trivial tune from mediocrity to drama.

CONCLUDING REMARKS

There are thousands of worthwhile musical compositions whose impact could be intensified, clarified, and enriched by a sensitive orchestrator. Many songs, chamber works, and piano and organ solos seem to require the all-encompassing range of orchestral expressiveness for the realization of their intrinsic idea, the essential motive of their creation.

Even the most renowned composers have not always presented their compositions in the medium that is wholly suited to their fullest realization. Orchestral composers, when writing for other media, rarely lose their orchestral concepts. Beethoven's piano sonatas and string quartets contain many passages that exceed the expressive capabilities of the indicated instruments. Many of Debussy's song accompaniments and piano compositions require that the pianist constantly attempt to produce the effect of contrasting textures and tone colors; and some of these pieces are so obviously orchestral that scoring them is a simple task.

When the indicated medium seems to fall short, the orchestra looms as the vehicle best suited to release a work's essential truth. No more perfect manifestation of the universal human musical instinct exists, and the basic sources of music—the inflections of speech and the pulsation of the human heart—have reached their highest point of refinement in the ensemble of orchestral instruments.

Even a cursory examination of nonorchestral literature will disclose a goodly number of works that lend themselves to orchestral treatment. Only the most highly idiomatic piano solos, those which depend for their success upon the peculiarities of the mechanics of pianistic technic, should be avoided. Although it is hardly feasible to score every page thus discovered to be a likely subject, it is an aid to the attainment of scoring skill to read through each new page with an eye and an ear to its instrumental possibilities.

Perhaps a melody, a texture, or some other suggestion of hidden richness in a simple composition will inspire the orchestrator to compose a more elaborate setting for it. The "Thanksgiving Song," page 288, is such an arrangement. The melody and general harmonic structure are familiar and established folksong ingredients: the disposition of accompaniment, the introduction and coda, and the sequence of their occurrence are the work of the arranger. A creative gift, and a thorough understanding of the technics of composition are required for this type of work, in addition to an ability to manage the instrumental ensemble.

Original composition for orchestra is a pastime that can be confidently engaged in only after gaining mastery of the technics of orchestration. The discipline required to score or arrange works whose purposes, moods, and personalities are already provided, is supplanted by a greater discipline, in which orchestration is fused with all other aspects of musicality. It is interesting to note the degrees of emphasis on orchestral skill exhibited in the orchestral compositions of the best-known composers. Some are examples of bread-and-butter scoring, and the orchestra is purely secondary; others are so brilliantly scored that their existence can hardly be imagined apart from their array of orchestral tones and textures.

Virtuosity is attained in orchestration, as it is in all musical undertakings, through serious study and constant practice. Even the most dazzling musical talent is inarticulate if its possessor is unable to cope with the mechanics of performance, and not a few limited talents have won wide acclaim as creative musicians through the intelligent employment of acquired skills.

No one is in danger of knowing too much about music. Nor is anyone in danger of knowing *all* about it. It is the author's hope that he has convinced the student of both these premises. A love and an understanding of orchestral music renders these truths not unpalatable, for the whole, full life of orchestral sound is but one exciting facet of the much greater mystery of all music.